Feedback From *My Manifesto* Clients

My manifesto sets me up for the day.
—Nicole (thirties)

I will continue considering and reflecting on many of the concepts and evolving my manifesto, as I realised this was the first time I had thought about many areas!
—Faith (twenties)

When I read my manifesto, I'm reminded of what is important.
—Joel (forties)

I really appreciated that throughout the book there was talk of not being perfect, of not putting pressure on myself to 'get it right', that there were no right answers ... I felt like it was okay to bring my full self to the process.
—Tunya (thirties)

Best thing I have ever done!
—Lisa (fifties)

The results are so powerful.
—Charlie (sixties)

I found the whole process really beautiful. For me, it was incredibly beneficial, grounding and recalibrating. I feel we all need a reminder sometimes of what is important and what is driving us, and this did it beautifully.
—Nic (forties)

It really was a gift to myself. I am proud of the manifesto I have created.
—Jo (fifties)

Published by Melbourne Books
Level 9, 100 Collins Street,
Melbourne, VIC 3000
Australia
www.melbournebooks.com.au
info@melbournebooks.com.au

Copyright © Sue Wong & Justin Robinson 2024

Title: My Manifesto: A compassionate guide
to reveal your best life
Authors: Sue Wong & Justin Robinson
ISBN: 9781922779212
Front cover design: Marianna Berek-Lewis
Book layout design: Ellen Cheng

All rights reserved. No part of this publication may be reproduced, stored in a retrieval system, or transmitted in any form or any means electronic, mechanical, photocopying, recording or otherwise without the prior permission of the publisher.

A catalogue record for this book is available from the National Library of Australia

Praise For *My Manifesto*

The world changed when Martin Luther nailed his Manifesto to the Castle Church doors in Wittenberg in 1517. Your world will change if you take the time to read, absorb and follow the guidance in this marvellous 'how to' manual for a better life. And you will not risk charges of blasphemy or ostracism, like Luther, but break from the shackles of the many layers of Ought Selves others have loaded onto you. Live your life to the fullest and use your Manifesto to jump start the process and declare it!

—**Richard Boyatzis**, co-author of international best seller, **Primal Leadership** and the new **Helping People Change**

Authors Robinson and Wong take us through a gradual process, in accessible, yet significant steps, that enable any one of us to create ... the kind of statement we have all longed for at one time or another. Their work, rooted in best practices in psychology, coaching, philosophy and their own lived experience, enables the reader to build an understanding of the self that is unique, powerful, and positive.

—**Maria Sirois**, author of **A Short Course in Happiness After Loss (and Other Dark, Difficult Times)**

The difference between living a full life (which many of us do in a constant state of busyness) and living life to the full (with all the richness, significance and variety that goes along with that) is so sharp it's almost frightening. Sue and Justin will help you move towards a better and valued way to bring your talents to the world, to your circle and – most importantly – to yourself.

—**Mark McKergow**, co-director of **The Centre for Solutions Focus at Work** and author of **The Next Generation of Solution Focused Practice and Host Leadership**

Gentle, inspiring and uplifting ... the world would be a much better place if we all went on this journey.

—**Hugh van Cuylenburg**, author of **The Resilience Project** and **Let Go**

The unique DIY approach taken in this book will prompt you to ask the big questions and then show you the small, doable steps, to create change. When you find your own inner gifts, you have more to give others. In this way *My Manifesto* is more than a simple book, it's an invitation to start a positive ripple effect.
—**Lea Waters**, **OAM**, author of ***The Strength Switch***

Justin and Sue's authenticity and positive collaboration shine throughout. I strongly recommend this book to those interested in further self-knowledge or a clearer life direction.
—**Chris Mackey**, author of ***The Positive Psychology of Synchronicity***

My Manifesto combines the most up-to-date science and ancient wisdom to provide a powerful and playful path to fulfillment and excellence. *My Manifesto* provides gentle, loving strategies for achieving and sustaining a beautiful life.
—**Robert Maurer**, author of ***One Small Step Can Change Your Life***

My Manifesto provides interesting and challenging ways to be part of a community where the synergy of many individuals can coalesce into a force for good.
—**Brigid Arthur**, coordinator of ***Brigidine Asylum Seekers Project***

Sometimes in life we know what we want but just lack the compass to get there. Simple, beautiful, and deeply meaningful; *My Manifesto* is a masterclass in self-discovery and personal empowerment.
—**Matthew Johnstone**, illustrator and author of ***The Big Little Book of Resilience*** and ***Stress Less***

My Manifesto is a brilliant guide to supporting us in living our best lives. I enjoyed the process of working through each of the steps to unlock some really powerful takeaways. Highly recommend the read.
—**Trent Cotchin**, author of ***From the Heart***

MY MANIFESTO

A compassionate guide
to reveal your best life

Sue Wong & Justin Robinson

M
MELBOURNE BOOKS

Disclaimer

Neither Sue nor Justin claim to be therapists. The information in this book is for self-education purposes. It is offered to aid self-coaching and, where relevant, to complement therapy or psychological advice. As you work through the book, should any situation arise for you, please consult with a therapist or health specialist of your choice.

This book is dedicated to mentors, authors, friends, coaches, and philosophers who have compassionately guided us to know and live our best lives.

It is our pleasure to offer you the opportunity to reveal your personal manifesto.

Sue Wong and Justin Robinson are distinguished career educators with extensive expertise in wellbeing education and growth coaching. Their profound knowledge has been honed through years of dedicated professional learning, coaching diverse clients, and engaging in continuous self-discovery. Their paths crossed at Geelong Grammar School, where Justin founded and directed the Institute of Positive Education, while Sue pioneered a highly successful coaching model. Together, they bring a wealth of experience and a refined 7-Step framework that reflects their commitment to empowering individuals on their journey towards personal and professional fulfillment.

Sue Wong

Sue has a Certificate IV and Diploma of Workplace and Business Coaching with Open Door Coaching. She is also a Professional Certified Coach with Growth Coaching International (GCI) in Leadership Coaching and Advanced Coaching: Solutions Focus Masterclass. She has her Coaching Accreditation with GCI. Sue's teaching qualifications include a BA Hons in English followed by a Dip Ed. Sue has deepened her ability to connect with students and teachers by adopting a coaching approach and pioneered a coaching model at Geelong Grammar School, which included developing coaches and introducing coaching concepts for teachers and students.

Justin Robinson

Justin has a Master of Education degree and a Certificate in Positive Psychology and an altMBA. He is an Honorary Fellow of the University of Melbourne's Graduate School of Education and is a global board member of the International Positive Education Network. In 2017, Justin was listed in The Australian Educator's Top 50 Hot List. He was the inaugural Director of the Institute of Positive Education, based at Geelong Grammar School, Australia. For more than ten years he was instrumental in pioneering a sustained implementation of Positive Education. He has also trained thousands of educators around the world in designing evidence-informed approaches to wellbeing.

CONTENTS

14	Introduction	

PART 1:   PRIMING YOUR MANIFESTO

20	Chapter 1:	Unique And Imperfect
28	Chapter 2:	The Gaining Of Wisdom
36	Chapter 3:	Starting Where You Are At
42	Chapter 4:	Questions As Doorways
49	Chapter 5:	Creative Living Beyond Fear
59	Chapter 6:	Our Pep Talk

PART 2:   CREATING YOUR MANIFESTO

70	Introduction to Part 2	
76	Chapter 7:	Step 1 – The Energising Step
99	Chapter 8:	Step 2 – The Courageous Step
120	Chapter 9:	Step 3 – The Mattering Step
138	Chapter 10:	Step 4 – The Visionary Step
154	Chapter 11:	Step 5 – The Releasing Step
177	Chapter 12:	Step 6 – The Connection Step
197	Chapter 13:	Step 7 – The Contribution Step
215	Chapter 14:	My Unique Manifesto

PART 3:   LIVING YOUR MANIFESTO

232	Chapter 15:	Your Pep Talk
243	Chapter 16:	Small Steps And Great Small Steps
251	Chapter 17:	Shaping Your Environment
258	Chapter 18:	Listening To Your Environment
266	Chapter 19:	Am I There Yet?

274	Acknowledgements
277	Appendices
277	Appendix 1: Frequently Asked Questions (FAQs)
280	Appendix 2: The VIA Classification Of Character Strengths
281	Appendix 3: An Overview Of Ten Key Positive Emotions
282	Appendix 4: Character Strengths 360 Exercise
283	Appendix 5: 50+ Authentic Living Books That We Love
284	Appendix 6: Some Inspirational Words

287	Sue's Current Manifesto
288	Justin's Current Manifesto

It is common to have a full life.

It is less common to live life fully.

Your manifesto can be the difference!

Sue Wong and Justin Robinson

Introduction

Hi!

We are excited to share with you what we have discovered, and have attempted to capture the essence of that discovery in this book. Our hope is that, in doing this, we will honour our compelling belief in servant leadership by compassionately guiding you to reveal your own manifesto – the statement that represents your best life.

Our 7-Step guide has been fine-tuned over years of personal discovery, hundreds of client coaching sessions, and has now been road-tested by individuals spanning from age twenty-one to eighty-four! It has proved relevant and empowering across genders, cultures, backgrounds, and life stages. This book acts as a DIY manual enabling you to craft your personal manifesto with confidence.

Developing and working through this process has been so good for us, and we have been told by our road-testers that it was good for them, too – so much so that we could not help but rush to share it with all of you. Your current, unique, and personal manifesto – a private declaration of wisdom and intentions – can also support you to live your best life and really help when you are feeling stuck or uncertain. We invite you to join us and seize this opportunity for personal growth and self-realisation.

To make this process as accessible as possible, we've arranged this book into three parts. In *Part 1: Priming Your Manifesto*, we get you ready for the upcoming 'work' in six related chapters that explain what a manifesto is, how it might help you, and some of the challenges you may come up against. You've got this!

In *Part 2: Creating Your Manifesto*, we take you through our curated 7-Step process as you complete relevant exercises and draft initial responses to seven powerful overarching questions. This is it. The good oil! We start up close and personal, *The Energising Step*, which is you revealing you, *to* you, and then we move to what you stand for. We call this *The Courageous Step* because it really takes courage to stand up and hold your ground for what is important to you. From there we progress to what you care about, *The Mattering Step*, and what you dream about, *The Visionary Step* – lovely stuff. Of course, having gone there, we've opened up the can of worms and out pops fear in *The Releasing Step*. We have to then release ourselves from it; enough of it, anyway, to be able to keep moving forward! Ah, and then we return to the lovely stuff again with a chapter on relationships, *The Connection Step*, and finish with *The Contribution Step*, in which we invite you to put into words what, ultimately, we all want, what we want being here to mean, what it was all about – our unique footprint.

We round off *Part 2* with the exciting and inspiring opportunity to bring all your work together as you reveal your manifesto, something we are sure will be a treasured document for you, full of your personal wisdom and insights.

We don't leave you here. You have your hard-won manifesto, now you need to live it! We therefore conclude our book with *Part 3: Living Your Manifesto*. This is where we explore the challenges and opportunities of harnessing, and living, your manifesto. We discuss the power of small steps, the importance of shaping and listening to your environment, and celebrating the joys and wonders of living life to the full. What a wondrous, celebratory part of the book this is! We hope you are smiling all the way through it.

We feel confident in the effectiveness of the process delivered in this book. Why? Because we followed it and we are living it! Not a day goes by that we don't feel grateful for the awareness that our manifestos have raised in us. Each day is a new chance to put into place all that we know that honours our unique, individual, short but rich time on this earth. Our confidence is further built by the positive experiences and feedback shared by our road-testers and our clients.

What have you got to lose? What have you got to gain?

We wish you well as you embark on this extraordinary journey of self-discovery. Create your personal manifesto, and live a life filled with authentic purpose and complete clarity.

You owe it to you.

With best wishes,

Sue & Justin

Sue & Justin

PRIMING
YOUR MANIFESTO

Chapter 1
Unique And Imperfect

Justin

To **know** yourself, to **care** for yourself, and to **believe** in yourself are three of the greatest gifts we can give to ourselves.

Thank you for putting your trust in us – this means a lot. Thank you for putting your trust in yourself – this means even more! We guarantee that this book will compassionately guide you through seven key steps to enable you to do the work of creating your personal manifesto. We guarantee that your manifesto will be unique. We guarantee that your manifesto will be imperfect. We guarantee that as you do the work, this book will truly become a gift to yourself. And finally, we guarantee that this gift to yourself will in turn become a gift to your loved ones and all the people you connect with in the days ahead. Are you ready to unwrap this gift?

The fact that you have a copy of this book in your hands and that you have made the commitment to read it tells us that you are ready. We truly believe that to know yourself, to care for yourself, and to believe in yourself are three of the greatest gifts we can give to ourselves. We do, however, wish to inform you that there is considerable work involved in unwrapping this gift. There will be times when you feel uncertain, and times when you are searching for responses.

You can think of your gift as being wrapped in seven layers of wrapping paper, with each layer representing one of the key questions we invite you to consider deeply, and to formulate a response. While this means it will take some time for you to unwrap your gift, it will be far easier than trying to unwrap something bound in a single thick, impenetrable layer.

Before we invite you to unwrap the first layer of this gift to yourself, we have dedicated six brief chapters to help you understand, appreciate, and treasure the gift that lies ahead. You can think of this section as nourishment to prepare and sustain you for the journey. So, let's begin the priming phase.

What Is A Manifesto?

It is interesting that the term 'manifesto' originates from two Latin terms: *manifestus,* meaning obvious and *manifesto,* meaning to make public. The early English term *manifest* also refers to making something clear to the eye or mind.

From these origins, what resonates with us are the references to making something 'clear', or obvious. This idea of bringing clarity to an important topic or subject is what we wish for you.

A more modern use of the term 'manifesto' has been the evolution to personal manifestos. In contrast to the current Oxford Dictionary definition of a manifesto as 'a public declaration of policy and aims', we think of a personal manifesto as 'a private declaration of wisdom and intentions'. Many clients we have worked with choose to display their manifesto within their homes and/or in their offices, still predominantly for their own inspiration, but also to inform and inspire close family members, friends, and colleagues. While it is non-negotiable for you to write down your declaration, the choice of how you wish to display your manifesto is deeply personal and something we will discuss in *Part 3* of this book.

Personal manifesto: a private declaration of wisdom and intentions.

As suggested by the title of this book, the major benefactor of this work is *you*. The understanding and expression of what is important to you will provide you with inspiration, direction, and a helpful decision-making framework.

Please know that a manifesto always focuses on a particular subject – in this case, the subject is *you*. Through our upcoming seven great questions, you will be guided to draw out your personal wisdom as you provide seven great responses, and then integrate these responses into a beautifully crafted personal manifesto.

Julian Hanna is a modern-day authority on manifestos. He is Assistant Professor at Madeira Interactive Technologies Institute in Portugal, and the author of *The Manifesto Handbook*.

In his book, Hanna draws on historical manifestos and suggests key tips for writing a good manifesto. Of relevance to our work, Hanna states that manifestos 'exist to challenge and provoke'. In our case, we hope the creation of your manifesto will challenge and provoke you in helpful and important ways.

To ensure your manifesto does challenge and provoke, you must feel safe and secure in the process. This is your book, your responses are personal to you, and you control how much or how little you wish to share with any significant others. We encourage you not to hold back in your thinking: if you need more room, find some extra paper. If you want to ponder or workshop your thoughts and responses, please do so.

Hanna also suggests that manifestos:

- usually include a list of tenets, principles, or beliefs;
- tend to embrace paradox and are theatrical;
- are better very short than very long.

We thank Julian Hanna for his in-depth research, and we encourage you to keep his rich insights in mind as you embark on creating your own personal manifesto.

Often physically slight and small in scale, **the manifesto is always grand in style and ambition.**

Julian Hanna

Your Manifesto Will Be Unique

We know you are unique and that there is no-one else quite like you. In fact, there will be thousands of ways you are unique, arising from your background, your upbringing, your environment, your experiences, your opportunities, your passions, your hobbies, your friends, and more! We invite you to treasure your uniqueness.

We also know that your manifesto will be unique. As you are guided through the seven steps, you will be asked to reflect upon specific questions, and not only will your responses reflect your unique personality, character, and personal wisdom, they will also reflect what deeply matters to you at your current age and stage of life.

We have no doubt if you were to revisit the seven steps to create your manifesto in just one or two years' time, there would be many similarities, but also important differences. We like to think of your manifesto as being stable and dynamic. For example, your manifesto may reflect stability in regard to your deeply held core values. On the other hand, your manifesto may reflect dynamism, as you grow in wisdom and as new experiences arise on your journey through life.

It is important that your manifesto contains *your* words – words that speak to you, words that provide you with a positive and enabling energy. We want you to feel entirely comfortable expressing your thoughts in your unique way.

Naturally, if we were to line up one hundred personal manifestos, we could expect the occasional repetition of an inspiring term, and the overlap of a similar theme. However, the formation and combination of *your* words, representing *your* story and journey will speak to you in a deeply personal and authentic way.

Your Manifesto Will Be Imperfect

We're all imperfect, and that's a good thing! We are not encouraging you to strive for perfection – in fact, the opposite. Yes, we wish for you to live authentically and to live intentionally, *and* we wish for you to be accepting of, maybe even comfortable with, your imperfections. Remember your imperfections also contribute to you being unique!

We most definitely want to release you from any misconceptions that your manifesto has to be 'perfect', or 'correct' – it will always be a work in progress for you, just as we are all ongoing works of progress.

Social research professor Brené Brown reminds us that striving to be our best or working toward excellence is healthy when it is internally driven. However, issues may arise when one is externally driven. Brown's research uncovered that perfectionism is generally externally driven by a simple but potentially all-consuming question: *What will people think?*

Perfectionism will become a barrier to the work we invite you to complete in creating your personal manifesto. We instead invite you to welcome in curiosity, to view your mistakes as opportunities for learning, and to view your imperfections as necessary elements of an authentic life.

We can't wait to support you as you embark on some of the most valuable work you have ever done. To further your preparation, in the next chapter Sue shares how you will gain wisdom as you do the work.

Questions We Invite You To Ponder

- In what ways are you unique?
- In what ways are you imperfect?

Chapter 2:
The Gaining Of Wisdom

Sue

An unexamined life **is not worth living.**

Socrates

I don't know about you, but for my whole life I have battled with questions around meaning and purpose. I was getting up in the morning and, for an awfully long time, going to work (forty-six years as a teacher), so I was purposeful enough and certainly loved doing what I was doing. But what did it all mean, and was I living *my* life? How was I to know?

I was raised within a faith and educated in a faith school. My experience of both was not to look too closely or question too much of what I was given, but to *accept* things as they were. I had trouble with that. I wanted to know *why*, and I wanted to see what other ways of living were out there.

So, as my life continued, I tested what I was given in many ways and stripped away a great deal of the inherited doctrines. I certainly created inner turmoil for myself. But I had to find my meaning and purpose, for as Socrates reputedly stated, 'An unexamined life is not worth living.' This tenet became my driver.

Being given so much, I must take a moment to express gratitude.

A definitive framework for living (according to the Bible, and compounded by my experiences of womanhood in the 1950s, being stripped of my voice) meant that for many years I just conformed. Until I didn't. The end result of that journey is a belief in myself (when I am feeling strong) and a determination to do it *my way* – thanks, Frank Sinatra!

First, I had to give myself permission to be me, to understand that I could stand toe-to-toe with others, and to construct my own meaning. The full force of that permission is a recent discovery for me.

I know, I am a slow learner, but I had to live a lot. Giving myself permission coincides with the process of working with Justin, during which time I read a great deal from the wellbeing circles he mixed in, absorbed those messages, embraced the concept of synchronicity, and developed with him **my manifesto**.

I concluded: it is absolutely crucial to know who I am and what I stand for, otherwise how do I know the life I am leading is *my* life? The method we devised to guide me, Justin, and *you*, is the seven steps in *Part 2* of this book.

How A Manifesto Can And Does Help

I would like to give a testimonial to how I now feel about having my manifesto: In times past I have felt overwhelmed by life's events, which were often out of my control. Now that I have done the work on my personal manifesto, I consciously know my true self and my best life. I am able to access my own wisdom through my carefully chosen words and can steady myself before choosing the best response – the one that serves me best among those which present themselves.

We also asked how our **my manifesto** mates felt their manifestos helped them. Here are some of their responses:

- 'I rise each morning and before I put a foot on the floor, I recite mentally the phrases of my personal manifesto. This sets me up for the day. I breathe deeply and am motivated to go about my day with purpose and intent.'
- 'When I read it, I take a big breath and exhale – and I'm reminded of what is important.'

- 'Best thing I have ever done. I no longer worry about the small stuff. My focus is on what matters the most.'
- 'Seeing my dreams and ideas in writing makes them feel more achievable and desirable.'
- 'I feel so blessed to have gone through the process and the results are so powerful! This is important work in the world, for individuals, their families, colleagues at work, and the wider community.'
- 'My manifesto provides me with a framework for decision-making. It reduces the angst of whether I am on the right track. If the decision I need to make fits with the self of my manifesto and allows me to live the life I have mapped out there, then it is the *right* decision for me. This eliminates the crisis of decision-making.'

We can feel just how much each of these mates is feeling empowered by having created their own personal, unique manifesto. Their energy is palpable. Your journey awaits you.

It is absolutely crucial to know who *I* am and what *I* stand for, otherwise how do *I* know the life *I* am leading is *my life*?

What Is Different In Our Lives Right Now?

It's a funny thing, but creating your personal manifesto, seeing it, reading it (daily, I suggest) somehow makes it seem more desirable and yes, more achievable. Why is that? Perhaps it is a case of seeing is believing. Just the fact that you have done the work, thought deeply, and chosen the best and most uplifting way to represent yourself and your life means that you've ended up with something very precious to you. And so it should be. It is *your* self and *your* story – unique and imperfect.

For me personally, I have discovered something very interesting. Having spent so many years thinking I was going to arrive at a time and place when I would be happy, and would have resolved all conflict (romance novels and Hollywood mythology have a lot to answer for), I realised that life was – another cliché – not about the destination, but about the journey. My personal manifesto is then the guide, the road map, for that journey.

You don't use a map once, unless you have memorised it; you consult it at every turn to make sure that you are still going the right way.

Having accepted that life always has the potential to be messy, and that there are times I will fall away from the best version of myself, I know **it is okay**. *I* am okay. I can always recalibrate. I have my True North and I have my compass. I am equipped for the journey. Bring it on! I am mostly calm, mostly in control, when I remember this. I have found my peace.

Family members have noticed and commented on the change in me. My son said, 'I have noticed how you have grown, and I want to grow, too.' And so began the ripple of my manifesto. He created – with the guidance that we have distilled for you in *Part 2* – his own personal manifesto. He now has the glorious satisfaction of charting his own course and celebrating his own wisdom. It is becoming increasingly evident to him – and to me – that he is now living his intentional life. The satisfaction I feel as a mum is incalculable.

It is in that spirit that we offer the 7-Step guide to you. Do yourself a favour; do the work and notice the results on your wellbeing.

I invite Justin to write his own observations here about what is different in his life since having his manifesto.

Are You A Zealot For Anything?

Thanks Sue, my short response is 'ditto'. Like you, I have benefited from using my manifesto as a gentle, compassionate guide, and the clarity of my words has contributed to a deep sense of inner peace.

My extended response is that my manifesto helps me to express my passions and inspires me to act in alignment with my values as I aspire to grow in wisdom and make a meaningful contribution to society.

I remember being asked in a job interview the specific question, 'Are you a zealot for anything?' My mind raced, sitting there in my navy suit, having spent the better part of an hour trying to sound articulate, confident, and composed. My immediate thought was that I had no idea what a zealot was! My second thought was that the term 'zealot' has a negative connotation and maybe my answer was meant to be a simple 'no' (later this negative association was partially confirmed, as I looked up the dictionary to see terms such as 'fanatical' and 'uncompromising' used to describe a zealot). However, my third and overriding thought was that the question was asked in such a way that the panel were looking for something that I was deeply passionate about – something that I would stand for.

As an aspiring educational leader, I eventually responded with, 'I'm a zealot for challenge!' I do believe deeply in trying to challenge myself and trying to challenge students within a safe and supportive learning environment.

I am not exactly sure where this passion came from, but over many years it has resulted in me embracing a range of physical, mental, social, and emotional challenges. While I have not succeeded in meeting all these challenges, they have all helped me to grow, to change. (I continue to smile at the quirky fact that if you take the first three letters and the last three letters of the word 'challenge' you arrive at the word 'change'!)

The reason I share this story is because my manifesto expresses my most important challenges and then it guides, excites, and nudges me in so many helpful ways. If I am ever asked this interview question again, I will also be adding that I am a zealot for creating personal manifestos!

Maybe at this stage you are beginning to feel nervous about starting your journey as you grapple with doubts that might be coming up for you. Read on to the next chapter, where we address the idea of fear.

Questions We Invite You To Ponder

- How will your life be better with your personal manifesto?
- How do you hope to grow throughout this process?

Our lives are better — so can yours **be.**

Chapter 3:
Starting Where You Are At

Sue

You have everything that you need *right now*.

It is important that you really believe you can – and should – begin your journey towards creating your written statement of who you are, what you stand for, and the life you're choosing to lead, from exactly the point of where you are now. Feelings such as *I am not good enough*, or *I will start after I have done this*, or *I will do this but first I have to* ... will only delay your start and potentially sabotage you from taking the journey at all. Recognise these self-imposed conditions for what they are – fear.

Many years ago, one of the wellbeing books that I read and have never forgotten (and the essence of which I use as a strategy in my life) is *Love Is Letting Go Of Fear* by Gerald Jampolsky. Essentially, he makes the case for love and fear being two polar opposites, so much so that they cannot co-exist in the mind at the same time. When we are in a state of love, there is no place for fear. Bringing love to mind when I am afraid frees me from the immobilisation of fear. I have a three-step strategy for this: recognise fear, sit within it, and summon love.

To **recognise fear**, the primal state, is the first step. If you can, do this early because the sooner you do, the sooner you can stop it from building.

Sit within it (presuming of course there is no *real* danger requiring immediate action) long enough for your pre-frontal cortex to begin to take control again, as it may be at least fifteen minutes before you can think logically.

Summon love. Bring to mind feelings of love – like a good method actor, derived from any context in your life that can be applied in the moment – and you begin to thaw.

You Are Enough

Through the process of creating my personal manifesto, I realised (and yes, it is always a matter of realising what, at a deep level, you know, have always known) that I am enough. While this is a relatively easy statement to write, believing it completely through all my layers of consciousness is not easy. I am tugged in and out of this awareness daily. I have restless nights and long, slow days (when I am in conflict, the day seems so long). But – and this is what we are offering you – when I come back to my manifesto, when I centre myself, I know again my reality: I am okay; I am enough.

We hope to deliver our message in a way that will reach you, and you, and you.

You see, we want *you* to hear our message. We want you to create *your* manifesto, to find your own peace (for me) and inspiration (for Justin). We have distilled the work to a 7-Step guide. We have given you tools to support you (*Part 2* of this book). We have equipped you to be independent on your journey – you don't need anybody else! However, for your interest, we have a companion website with additional resources, and we've also provided a range of ways you can engage with this work, including online coaching sessions and in-person retreats.

This is our assurance to you: whoever you are, wherever you are, you are enough, and you have enough to do this work; you don't have to have an academic degree to understand and apply this work. Delivering this message is our mission in writing this book. Know *you* are welcome as you are. So, start right there: *where you are at*.

And You Can Grow

Having said that – you are welcome just the way you are – it is also important for you to know that doesn't mean this is the way you want to stay. After all, life is about growth and continuous learning.

It is, however, important to start the journey with an open heart and a growth mindset. Open-heartedness sounds simple, but to achieve it requires vulnerability and takes courage to adopt. From the snapshots of my life that I've shared with you, you will understand that personal safety has been my default since childhood. *You see, you can't get hurt if you don't open yourself. If you don't try, you can't fail. If you don't go outside your comfort zone, you won't exceed your capabilities.* All true, but boring and shrinking.

You stay safe, but you also don't grow.

Open-heartedness can be learnt, like all behaviour. If, like me, it does not come naturally because you are very good at protecting yourself, you can intentionally, little by little, practise opening your heart every day. To open your heart to do the work with us requires trust: trust in us, that we are offering you something of value, but more importantly in yourself. You do have your answers and you can do it if you try. Give yourself permission – take a calculated risk.

The beauty about our invitation is that you can do the seven steps in your own time, in your own way, in your own chosen environment. The effects of your work, when applied, will be noticed – in a good way. You can, however, choose whether to display your personal manifesto or to keep it entirely for yourself. After all, this is *your* business.

We invite you to adopt a growth mindset, where you are open to change and open to improving your mental stance. Growing up in the 1950s, female and Catholic, I was taught how to develop a fixed mindset. I did everything I could to amass knowledge. I was a very compliant, (initially) high-achieving child. Once I had some knowledge, I held it very closely and used it to feel good about myself and, to be even more honest, to feel superior to others.

To change this way of being is a challenge. Being open to change, being open to growth, being willing to share it with others, may seem to risk your power base, but there is no need to come from a scarcity paradigm. We now know, thanks to scientific advancement, about neuroplasticity. We have the capacity for unlimited accumulation of knowledge. So, rather than protect the little that we do know, we can add more and new knowledge over the course of our lifetimes! What needs to change is therefore not our physiology, but our attitude. So please bring to your work in the seven steps a beginner's mind – one that is evergreen and pliant, and empower yourself as I, Justin, and all our manifesto mates have done. Unwrap your gift.

The vulnerability you feel when you open your heart is your **humanity on display.**

Where Are You At?

We haven't left you on your own for this journey. In *Part 1*, we are priming you for the upcoming work, providing you with important information and inspiration. We then give you many helpful strategies within the seven key steps discussed in *Part 2* of this book. Then, in *Part 3,* we focus on how to live the life of your personal manifesto.

For now, we need you to know that this process will meet you where you are at. Our company **my manifesto** logo aims to artistically combine the letter 'm' with the vision of a journey (and indicate a ripple effect).

On the diagram below we have placed several dots to represent different points that people who are reading this book may be at.

Whoever you are, whichever dot may represent you, allow us to lead you towards growing an understanding of yourself. In doing so, you will be acting out the historical wisdom of the oracle inscribed on the walls of the temple at Delphi: *Know Thyself*. We continue in the next chapter with these questions as a doorway …

Questions We Invite You To Ponder

- Where are you at?
- When have you embraced vulnerability in the past?

Chapter 4:
Questions As Doorways
Sue

Answers are closed rooms; and **questions are open doors** that invite us in.

Nancy Willard

There is so much written about the question. I particularly like the concept of the question as a doorway. A doorway is a way in, an entry point to the room, the home, the building. For our work, labelling questions as doorways makes the point that the question is the entry point into your 'room', your inner life.

Answers are closed rooms. Once an answer has been provided, it tends to shut the conversation down. If you have been in that conversation, in which someone is looking for the opportunity to provide all the answers, you know how off-putting that can be. I always wondered what the Buddhists meant by 'love the question'. I take it to mean that the question has the power to open up rooms rather than close them down. As more questions occur to you, thinking continues. As soon as an answer arrives, it tends to close the door on that room. Why not keep the door open a little longer and see what arises? You may surprise yourself.

The point of a question in this coaching context is to **open up your conversation with you**, rather than to close it down.

You Are Coaching You

The essence of the coaching approach is to ask the question and wait for the answer rather than advise or tell. The reason for this is that if the coach advises or tells, they may never know what the coachee's answer may be. There is also a power inequality to it; in this model, the one who is advising is presumed to know more. This approach shrinks most people into giving an appeasing answer, and in the worst-case scenario, when that happens, the coachee will think it is the *wrong answer*.

Remember, in the work towards creating your personal manifesto, there is no wrong answer, only *your* answer which is the best answer for you. This is why a coaching approach is a natural fit for your personal manifesto journey.

The obvious difference here is there is no external coach. You must coach you! That is why we have distilled our lived experience, our reading, and our experience of working with clients over the years into the seven steps of this book. We want you to succeed. We invite you to be guided by us to develop your unique manifesto.

Gauging by the feedback from our clients, you will see yourself reflected on the page and feel the power that comes from seeing your vision for *your* life – the one you have coached into being.

Before you go on …

Two terms I would like to mention here are Positive Energy Attraction (PEA) and Negative Energy Attraction (NEA). When you are coaching yourself, it is really important to notice how particular words make you feel. You know how it feels when you are having a conversation and a word is used that shuts you down? That word or expression has a NEA for you. The same thing can happen when you are coaching yourself if you choose a word or expression which has that effect.

We can pick this point up again when you are working on your personal manifesto words. For now, I just want you to be aware of the effect that certain words can have on your emotions when answering the questions. If they lift you, then they have PEA. If they shut you down, then they have NEA. Change them! Don't discourage yourself! And read on for one of the most powerful questions you may ask yourself.

A Word And A Question

An inspiring and helpful question you can ask as a coach is also AWE, which in coaching circles stands for 'And What Else?' While this question may have some NEA for you, because it represents more work, the word itself, 'Awe', is on our inspiring words list and so it has a PEA effect! This seemingly simple question added to any line of inquiry that you may be pursuing, keeps the door open! So, when you are pondering the questions in our seven steps and have been using your skills of waiting patiently and self-compassionately for your answer, affirming and encouraging yourself for your efforts, *before* you leave that space to go on to the next step, ask the question, 'And what else …?' This encouragement is designed to bring out any additional thoughts that you might have. Most often, our first thoughts are not necessarily our best thoughts, and they are never our only thoughts. This question will prolong your conversation with yourself, but it might also turn up gold.

So, rather than closing the doors on a question as soon as you feel you have an answer, instead:

- wait;
- ask AWE three times;
- and see what answer arises.

These are the answers which will provide the content to select from when drafting your personal manifesto.

The AWE question will prolong your conversation with yourself, **and it might also turn up gold.**

A Word Of Caution

By the way: don't step into the space we have created for you only to become an advisor to yourself. Continue to be an inquirer. Maintain the gentleness and curiosity of a friend in your questioning, wait for the ideas to flow, encourage yourself to continue, and affirm your efforts with praise and without judgement when they come. It is all-too easy to get in your own way, to listen to the voices we all have in our heads, and to sabotage yourself.

Before I go on, just an aside …

In this world we live in, we all get knocked around by the demands, challenges, *and* criticism which are part of our everyday. Don't add to the negativity by criticising yourself! Often, we are our own harshest critics. Instead, treat yourself like you would a good friend.

Dr Kristen Neff is known internationally for her self-compassion work. Look into her work further for great ideas and exercises if you recognise that you need to work on this area. For our purposes here, know this: you are worthy of the compassion that you would freely give to your friend. Be a friend to you.

I was first attracted to coaching after reading Sir John Whitmore's pioneering work, *Coaching for Performance*. What was so powerful for me was the relative simplicity (as often the most profound ideas are) of the central idea that coaching is about raising awareness and then allowing responsibility to follow. And awareness is best raised through questioning.

What your task is, then, is to bring what you know to the surface of your mind so that you are aware of it and then to take *responsibility* for it by living your life intentionally.

The 7-Step process is all about raising your awareness. By the end of it, you'll be ready to take up the responsibility. We assist you with ways to do that in *Part 3* of this book.

To raise your awareness in the seven steps, we needed questions that would cause you to stop, think, and respond. Our search was then directed toward the powerful questions to do this. We believe the questions and exercises we arrived at create the buzz of the work.

As an aside, we invite you to refer to our list of 'authentic living books' we love at the back of this book (see Appendix 5) if you would like to explore any of this work further.

Questions We Invite You To Ponder

- What question would you like to ask yourself?
- How can you be a great coach to yourself?
- How can you remain curious?

Chapter 5:
Creative Living Beyond Fear

Justin

Your personal manifesto can assist you to **live a life** more strongly **driven by connection** than by fear.

In general, we don't fear routine, but we do fear change. We don't fear the known, but we do fear the unknown; we don't fear sitting in an audience, but we do fear speaking in front of an audience. Why do we fear change, the unknown, and public speaking? Because we are hard-wired to protect ourselves.

As humans, we are hard-wired to connect with others *and* hard-wired to protect ourselves, and sometimes these two wirings come into conflict with one another. As a social species, humans have evolved to coordinate their needs, thoughts, and feelings with others. It was only within a group that our ancient ancestors were able to survive, and hence much of our brain activity is devoted to reading the intentions of others and finding a way to fit in and be accepted. Fascinatingly, neuroscientists have found that social rejection actually triggers the physical pain centres in our brains.

Many of you will be familiar with our 'flight-fight-or-freeze' response, which is our body's response to threat. This confirms how 'wired' we are to protect ourselves, and this threat response is extremely powerful and extremely helpful when we are facing a real physical threat – our breathing and heart rate increases so we can get more oxygenated blood to our muscles and brain, our pupils dilate to optimise our sight, and our muscles tense in preparation.

So, if our brains are built for survival and if we are wired to minimise or move away from threats to avoid danger, we can see how we may be tempted to live a 'safe' life. This could be viewed as attempting to live a life void of fear. While this makes some sense on a physiological level, it makes *less* sense when a lot of our fears are simply in our heads (in our thoughts), and may potentially rob us from living fully.

The title of this chapter is borrowed from Elizabeth Gilbert's empowering book *Big Magic – Creative Living Beyond Fear*. As you prepare to work through the 7-Step process to create your manifesto, we want you to embrace the concept of 'living beyond fear'. Let's look a little deeper into what this means.

In *Starting Where You Are At*, Sue shared her three-step plan for freeing herself from what she referred to as her experience of 'the immobilisation of fear'. Sue's three steps were: Recognise fear, Sit within it, and Summon love.

Sue's three steps have definitely assisted me at times when fear has played loudly in my mind. Firstly, to recognise my thoughts for what they are – fear! It makes sense, due to our wiring, that we should be experiencing fear when we try something new, when we put ourselves out there, when we endeavour to live fully. Experiencing fear isn't the problem and it isn't something we should be trying to avoid – it's just that we wish to move beyond that feeling of fear. Our hope is that, rather than seeking to retreat and escape the emotion of fear, we accept and even embrace it, or as Sue wisely prescribes in her second step, *Sit within it*. And then, after sitting within and beside your feelings of fear, realising that you are okay, you can summon thoughts and feelings of love. These thoughts can, and should, include self-love and self-compassion. Summoning love can also include visualising feelings of warmth and care from wholehearted loved ones.

Understanding *It's* Coming

We would like to make very clear that fear will show up for you. In some ways, and please don't take this the wrong way, we *hope* it shows up for you! Why, you may ask? Well, because if you feel elements of fear, this is a strong guide that you are on to something that is important to you, something that matters to you. This is no longer just a theoretical exercise; this is real, this is your life.

Once you know *it's* going to happen, then you can prepare yourself and consider ways to manage fear effectively. We suspect it happens to every single person, even though we don't talk about it much. I shared with Sue the other day how much my legs can shake just before I give a talk. Sue had no idea – she was surprised – because in some external way it 'looked like' I had it all together as I went on to deliver my talk. We know so little about what is going on inside the minds and bodies of others, but it is safe to assume that it's probably pretty similar to what is going on inside your own mind and body. There is self-doubt, there is negative self-talk, and there is, more often than not, fear!

Liz Gilbert, in her book *Big Magic,* uses the powerful metaphor of 'The Road Trip' to help us make space for our fears. In her metaphor she refers to 'fear' as one of her family members who is welcome to come along for the ride, because she knows they always will, but that fear must sit in the back seat, not suggest detours, not adjust the temperature, and not even choose the songs on the stereo!

When you feel fear creeping in, there is no need to ignore it and no need to push through it. Instead, step back, breathe, and remember that your own mind and body have created this fear to help you.

Knowing that fear is a part of living authentically puts us in a far stronger position to be able to manage it, embrace it, or as some like to think of, 'dance with it'.

Passion Can Overcome *It*

Please close your eyes for a moment (well, not just yet) and think of someone you know who is exceedingly passionate about something. Maybe they are passionate about their family, their work, a particular hobby, or a particular charity. Maybe they are passionate about donating blood, or passionate about a particular social issue. Visualise them performing or participating in their passion. (You can go ahead and close your eyes, now.)

Was some form of fear present? If there was, the evidence shows that they were out there, they were doing what they loved, they were having a go. Do you think it could be fair to say, then, that their passion had overcome their fear?

Passion engenders courage because you are driven to realise something that is deeply important to you, and your sense of purpose becomes more powerful than your sense of fear. Parents may be familiar with overcoming personal fears to support their children, and this was due to the passion they have for their family.

We suggest that an incredibly important thing for you to be passionate about is *you*. While supporting your favourite sporting team may feel important, surely it can't be as important as supporting yourself! (Of course, these two need not be mutually exclusive.)

Fear can be a dream killer; it can become our silent (or internal) voice that pushes us to lose our passion in a vain attempt to seek safety for ourselves. Sure, a possible alternative is to dream smaller dreams that potentially incite less fear, but we would strongly encourage you to dream freely and fully and then to move beyond the fear when it shows up.

'**Dearest fear**, ... I acknowledge that you believe you have an important job to do in my life, and that you take your job seriously. Apparently, your job is to induce complete panic whenever I am about to do anything interesting – and, may I say, you are superb at your job.'

Liz Gilbert, **Big Magic,** *an excerpt from 'The Road Trip'*

Passion can overcome fear – the fear of losing, of failing, of being traditional.

Seth Godin

Moving Beyond It

We worry that some people think positive emotions are 'good' and negative emotions are 'bad', and therefore the goal is to experience as many positive emotions as possible, and to avoid, or push away, or suppress, any negative emotions. This is not only incorrect, but also unhelpful and harmful. Humans will and should experience a full range of positive and negative emotions as part of living a rich, full, and meaningful life.

Acceptance and Commitment Therapy (ACT) is a form of behaviour therapy that assists people to effectively manage negative emotions. The goal of ACT is to create a purposeful life, while accepting the pain that inevitably goes with it.

Scientific studies have shown ACT to be effective in a wide range of clinical conditions, including depression, workplace stress, chronic pain, anxiety, OCD, drug abuse, and PTSD.

ACT teaches mindfulness skills as an effective way of handling the private experience of negative or unpleasant emotions. Two of these skills are 'Defusion' and 'Expansion' and they have helped us, and we believe you may find them useful also.

Fusion is the opposite of Defusion. Fusion is where we are fused to our thoughts – we consider our thoughts to be the literal truth: they must be obeyed and require our full attention. When we fuse with our fear, it has an enormous influence over our behaviour.

Defusion means we can step back and observe our thoughts without being caught up in them. We can recognise that our thoughts are nothing more, or nothing less, than an ever-changing stream of words and images. If we can defuse our thoughts, they have much less power or impact over us.

For example, if you are having a fearful thought, such as a fear of failure:

'I can't _____ , I'm not _____ enough.'

In the first blank, insert whatever it is you want to do – start a business, complete a degree, write a book, go out on a date. In the second blank, insert whatever your fear is, what you believe you are not – funny, smart, attractive, strong, brave enough.

One of many possible Defusion techniques is simply noticing that you are having this thought. So, you simply say to yourself, 'I notice I am having the thought that …', and if the thought repeats itself regularly, you can go on with, 'There it is again, I notice that I am having that thought that …'

This process of changing your relationship with the thought can help to bring welcome distance and reduced intensity and impact.

Expansion is one way of helping us to accept negative emotions. The purpose of this technique is to make room for unpleasant feelings and sensations and allow them to come and go without struggling with them or giving them undue attention.

In returning to my shaky legs prior to speaking in public, while I would prefer this automatic response didn't happen, I find the less I fight it, and simply breathe into the response, the less it hinders me. It may feel counter-intuitive, and it can be common for me to do the opposite – to try to push away fear, or any nerves and unwelcome sensations – as I prepare to speak in public. Quite often, though, because I am consequently on the lookout for such responses and try to actively suppress and fight them, what actually happens is that the response becomes worse.

The Expansion alternative is for me to notice how I am feeling, to acknowledge that speaking in public about something that matters to me causes me some anxiety, but that this is okay, and I can breathe deeply into my body and observe a level of calm. And, even if my legs shake a bit, I can still effectively deliver my message, and not even Sue will know that my legs were shaking!

We hope you will approach your personal manifesto with this acceptance of fear, and with the courage that exists within you to bring forth your uniqueness, your creativity, and your treasures.

Yes, exercise your courage to move beyond fear.

Yes, exercise your curiosity to discover, and possibly rediscover, what matters.

Yes, exercise your self-compassion as you lovingly open possibilities.

We hope this exploration of fear has settled any nerves you may have been experiencing. We now turn our attention to our final priming chapter where we review the key messages we've covered so far, express our guarantees to you, and explain why we call it 'the work'.

Questions We Invite You To Ponder

- What are you fearing?
- Which of these fears make sense and may be worth keeping?
- Which of these fears do you wish to move beyond?

Chapter 6:
Our Pep Talk

Justin

Your future is in good hands ... *yours*!

When you read the title of this chapter, did you get excited for your final pep talk before running through the banner and into *Part 2* of this book? Or maybe you read the title and thought, *I'm not sure I need a pep talk; let's just get on with the seven steps – the last thing I need is some high-energy ranting and raving from Sue and Justin.* Or are you somewhere in the middle?

We like the term 'pep', and we do hope this chapter puts a bit of 'pep', a bit of energy and liveliness, into your step as you approach the seven steps.

We will leave it up to you. If you want to have your headphones on and play a particular inspiring song in the background as you read this, or whether you are enjoying the peace of mind that is already presenting itself, we hope you find your own way to appreciate the centring calm of this work.

What's Happened So Far

Justin's acceptance of Sue's coaching offer became the catalyst for a symbiotic partnership that led to a service called **my manifesto**, which has now been extended into a co-written book. We are not offering you anything that we have not trialled first. *We are living our lives each day as a result of these teachings.* Now, we want to gift it to you, but realise too that, really, you will gift yourself with it ... if you open it.

In *Unique and Imperfect,* we reminded you that you are unique and imperfect, and so your personal manifesto will be unique and imperfect too! It will be authentic to you, though. We encouraged you to embrace your imperfections and to acknowledge them as a universal part of the human condition (in other words, no-one is perfect!).

We know that the trip will have its tough moments, as well as its amazing ones – just like life, really! We defined your personal manifesto as 'a private declaration of wisdom and intentions', which you can keep that way, or shout it from the rafters. It's up to you. You are the subject of your manifesto. It is a celebration of you. While your manifesto may seem small in scale, we know on good authority that it will be grand in style and ambition. It is 'stable and dynamic'; some things within it may never change but remain essential to you. Others may alter with the ebb and flow of your life. So, revise!

The Gaining Of Wisdom was about the wisdom you gain by living. We answered the question, 'How can a personal manifesto help?' We provided testimonials from our **my manifesto** mates who attest to the positive effect it has had on their lives.

Your written expression identifies your life's direction and guides your decisions along the way. Living this identified life intentionally, we believe, is the key to a fulfilled life. A peaceful life. A hope-filled life. An inspired life. A passionate life. A happy life.

A bonus, too – the effect of you living your life in this way ripples outward to all who you share your life with. They will feel your energy, they will want to take the journey, too, and the world will be a better place because of all of us.

Starting Where You Are At reassured you that you can start this journey *today!* It can begin where you are now as you already have everything that you need. We asked you to accept yourself, recognise fear for the self-limiting emotion that it is, and proceed in all your vulnerability. We invited you to adopt a growth mindset and open your heart to experience the joy that will flow from really knowing yourself and living your life intentionally.

Questions As Doorways explained the fundamental tools for your manifesto journey are the questions which we provide. We view questions as the doorways into the rooms of your inner life. We invited you to open up to yourself in robust inquiry and coach your manifesto into being. We cautioned you not to sabotage and criticise yourself along the way, but to go gently when gaining your insights. The challenge is to become aware of what you know, because from that awareness, your responsibility will flow. You take up that responsibility every time you choose your action in keeping with your awareness.

In *Creative Living Beyond Fear,* we devoted a whole chapter to fear, as it is so influential in our lives. And therefore, *understanding* its role and place in our lives is so important. Our need to protect ourselves – an evolutionary hard-wiring – can come into conflict with our need to connect. We advocated recognising fear and embracing it in order to live a full life beyond fear. Fear is your indicator that you are in important territory. You care! But an exciting discovery we shared with you is that *passion* minimises, and maybe even overcomes fear! We invited you to get passionate about you.

It's Almost Time

It is almost time; you are almost ready to do 'the work'! Just one final pep talk from us and you are on your way. In our last chapter we discussed moving beyond fear in such a way that we can uncover and release the treasures that lie within. Another way of helping us move beyond fear is to understand the common human regrets, and view living authentically as a way of avoiding such disappointments.

Bronnie Ware is a name you might not be familiar with. She is an Australian nurse who worked for many years in a palliative care setting, supporting people in the final stages of their life. Her international best-selling book, *Top Five Regrets of the Dying* is based on the 'lessons and life-changing insights' she was offered 'while sitting by the bedsides of dying people as their carer and listener.'

Can you guess what the most common regret was? It certainly wasn't that people had wished they'd gone bungee jumping or made more money. And it wasn't that they hadn't stayed in closer contact with old friends – that was number four! The most common regret of all was that they didn't have the courage to live a life true to themselves, rather than the life others expected of them.

When we read this, we felt deeply saddened by the realisation that the thing people most wished they could go back and change about their lives was the one thing, perhaps more than anything else, that had always been within their control. The same one thing that we have within our control every moment throughout our life: The freedom to make decisions and choices that reflect who we are at our core – that reflect our most deeply held values.

Why We Call It 'The Work'

In *Questions As Doorways,* Sue introduced the two terms of PEA and NEA, referring to how a word, phrase or question can have a Positive or Negative Energy Attraction which may vary from individual to individual.

For us, 'the work' has a PEA. It helps us to think about rolling up our sleeves and getting into it. It helps us to prioritise our time and reminds us that this is not just something nice to do – this is important, this is work! The endeavour of writing a personal manifesto does require work – work in terms of energy, effort, and commitment. For us, it has been extremely meaningful and purposeful work.

Sometimes we work by ourselves and sometimes we work with others. This 'work' involves considerable personal reflection time but can also thrive with some teamwork when you engage with others to uncover further insights and wisdom. Yes, this work is predominantly mental work, and does not require physical labour, but don't underestimate the value of a brisk walk or some physical exercise to break and energise your mental labour.

We hope you are looking forward to doing the work. It shouldn't feel like a chore, and if it does, take a break, possibly change your environment, or put it down for a period of time. And of course, remember Sue's words from *Questions As Doorways*: if a phrase has NEA for you, then feel free to change it! So, if you would prefer to think of the work as your adventure, or 'me time', or anything that encourages you to set aside dedicated time to explore the seven steps, then please go for it!

Some Last Minute Tips

- Schedule time to do the work.
- Find a safe and comforting place to do the work.
- As you do the work, go easy on yourself.
- Trust in the process of doing the work.
- Trust in yourself to have all that you need to do the work right now.
- When and if it feels right, share and discuss the work with loved ones.
- Enjoy the work.

Questions We Invite You To Ponder

- When will you do this work?
- Where will you do this work?
- What will you refer to this work as?

Our Guarantee*

We guarantee that these seven steps will:
- stop you doubting yourself;
- provide you with a trouble-free life;
- eliminate negative emotions in your life;
- ensure life is fair to you;
- remove fear from your life;
- create a perfect you and a perfect life;
- make you happy.

* Please know that the above list is actually NOT at all what we guarantee!

We believe it is not possible for anyone, or any program, to guarantee such things, and even more importantly, we don't think living authentically is possible without experiencing the opposite of the above items.

Life wouldn't be life if all the above things were stripped away. We don't want you to create a perfect you or a perfect life or a perfect manifesto.

So, what is it we actually guarantee? Please see the next page for our *real* guarantee.

Our Real Guarantee

We are confident that these seven steps will:
- minimise internal conflict;
- help you navigate life;
- build hope;
- raise your awareness of what is important to you;
- provide greater clarity in your life;
- uncover rich personal insights;
- assist you to make difficult decisions.

It's time! Time for you to uncover your best self, and to live a life true to you. **We believe in you!**

2

CREATING YOUR MANIFESTO

Introduction To Part 2

In *Part 2* of this book, we use a coaching approach to support you in drawing out the content to create your personal manifesto. Before you embark on the seven steps, we would like to explain several key features that you will come across on a consistent basis.

A central question to ponder.
Within each step, we pose one central question for you to consider. Intentionally, we unpack each question, allowing you to focus on specific words as you begin to ponder your response.

Three exercises to consider.
We have designed three exercises for you to complete within each chapter. These exercises invite you to explore essential elements of the step and will provide you with rich insights to the central question. Please note that the exercises are stand-alone opportunities to stimulate your thinking. Though aspects of your responses to these exercises may appear in your manifesto answers, this does not have to be the case.

An AWE opportunity.
Within each chapter, we ask you the AWE question (And What Else?). This is such a simple, yet powerful, question. When prompted, you may find you have additional thoughts that you would like to record. From our experience, we find people often have something else they wish to add.

Case studies to enjoy.
You will find these at the back of each chapter. The case studies are taken directly from others who have completed the seven steps and graciously provided us with their permission to share. They are included simply for your interest; refer to them as little or as much as you feel is helpful. Some of you may see them as spoilers and only refer to them when you have finished your own version. That is fine, too! They do not serve as models, so please do avoid making comparisons upon which you judge yourself and others. Remember we have featured diverse people from different walks of life and stages of personal growth. Please note that the case studies represent individuals from their twenties to their seventies across a diverse range of occupations and life circumstances. No one person's complete manifesto is revealed in full – rather, we have featured several responses for each of the seven steps in an attempt to demonstrate the many versions we received. The word length varies greatly, chosen by the creator to suit their needs. We prefer no one way over another; each has the unique validity of its creator.

Your draft response.
At the end of each step, you will be invited to write down your 'answer' to the central question. We do require you to put in a response, but you don't need to think of it as formal or fixed. We encourage you to simply get onto paper your draft response and just sit with it for a period of time.

Each step involves:
- A central question to ponder.
- Three exercises to consider.
- An AWE opportunity.
- Case studies to enjoy.

Each step concludes with:
- Your draft response to the central question.

Other Things To Consider

Writing or recording?
Space is provided in this book for you to write down your responses, and please know you are not just welcome, but encouraged to dirty this book: dog-eared pages, notes written in margins, sticky-notes, highlighters, underlining; they are all so welcome.

On our website we also provide a range of document templates that you can download and print – this is another way you may wish to complete the exercises. Some people prefer to keep their own personal journal beside them as they work through the book and complete their exercises and responses directly in their journal.

It is common for thoughts to come to you throughout your day as you do this work. So, you may wish to keep a notepad with you, or type a note on your phone. Some people have enjoyed recording voice memos on their phone as they work, or walk, or wait. Please capture and store your thoughts however best suits you.

Fast or slow?
We provide no recommendation regarding the ideal rate you should progress through the seven steps. We believe you will know the rate that feels 'just right' to you. The fastest we have heard someone complete the work is in one day, where they viewed it like a retreat and set aside the day to reflect deeply on each of the steps in turn. Others have taken seven days or seven weeks. And others have simply chipped away and made progress when the opportunity arose and the environment felt right for them to consider what is deeply important to them. You know our response; please do whatever feels right for you.

P.S: But make sure you do them! No putting this important work off – they are just draft responses, anyway!

Bringing it all together
In the final chapter of *Part 2*, having completed the necessary preparations from the seven steps, we then guide you through the process of bringing all your work together. There are opportunities to refine your draft responses, specific questions for you to consider, and the final task of crafting your current, unique, personal manifesto.

Exciting times ahead, but for now your work is simply to turn the page and embrace *Step 1: The Energising Step.*

Go well!

7 The Contribution Step

6 The Connection Step

5 The Releasing Step

4 The Visionary Step

3 The Mattering Step

2 The Courageous Step

1 The Energising Step

Chapter 7

Step 1: The Energising Step

Justin

Character Strengths allow us to **believe in ourselves** and to **believe in others**.

What's wrong with you? I thought I might start here, with a phrase you may have heard said to you, or a phrase I may have said in an exasperated tone to myself or to someone else. Mind you, I suspect that you might be thinking this doesn't feel like a great start to our energising step!

One of the reasons we know there's something wrong with us is that we *all* have an innate, in-built negativity bias – we can't help but focus on what is wrong with us, and what is wrong with others. We have an inherent tendency to dwell on what could go wrong, and to ruminate on our mistakes and our flaws.

What's right with you? It is time to be energised, because we think it is vitally important for *all* people to also know what is right with them! You are about to receive a new language about what is right with humans; this is the language of Character Strengths.

You will quickly feel familiar with this new language, and you will be invited to complete several exercises so that by the end of this step you will be able to respond, with great clarity, to the following energising question.

The Energising Question

'What are my Signature Character Strengths?'

What we need is a tool to help us understand and celebrate what is right with us! This tool can balance, complement, and even overcome our sometimes destructive and paralysing negativity bias! This tool is actually not just one tool but a set of twenty-four tools known as our Character Strengths.

Character Strengths are the positive human qualities that, when used effectually and morally, support us to bring good into our world. These universal tools support us to live a good life. We view these strengths of character as the fuel to drive our skills and talents.

* In Appendix 2 you will find the list of the twenty-four VIA Character Strengths accompanied by their formal definitions.

What are my Signature Character Strengths?

What: We are looking for a list of items. We provide you with a recognised classification to assist you in this process.

My: This is all about your qualities, and it comes down to your actions and behaviours.

Signature: Referring to your top or highest Character Strengths. Just like it is now effortless and natural for you to write your signature, drawing upon your Signature Strengths should be similarly effortless and natural.

Character Strengths: These are the positive human qualities that exist within you.

Discovering and accepting that I had strengths brought a deep sense of calm. **Knowing I had these inner resources available to me at all times in any situation helped me find self-security for the first time in my life.** I realised that my strengths weren't just a life raft when the sea was choppy, they were also the oars that could help me row toward a more positive shore.

Lea Waters

Character Strengths Principles

1. Universally valued.
Each of the twenty-four VIA Character Strengths is morally valued across different cultures and religions. They are also respected and valued in our society today.

2. Exist within each of us.
While some Character Strengths may be more comfortable for individuals to use, all twenty-four do exist within each individual and can be drawn upon to action.

3. Stable and dynamic.
It is important to understand that while an individual's character is relatively stable, it is certainly not a fixed state of their being, and it is common to notice shifts in character over time.

4. Possible to grow.
Anyone can choose to develop and nurture a particular Character Strength through intentionally actioning it on a more regular basis.

5. Potential shadow-side.
It is important to recognise that you can underuse, overuse, or misuse your Character Strengths. The Goldilocks principle of just the right amount is relevant here.

Exploring Our Signature Strengths

We refer to our top strengths, the ones we most commonly and skilfully action, as our 'Signature Strengths', our middle strengths as our 'Familiar Strengths', and our lesser strengths as our 'Supporting Strengths'.

Three E words can help us identify if we think a Character Strength qualifies as a Signature Strength: **e**ssential, **e**ffortless, and **e**nergising.

A Signature Strength should feel essential to who you are; without it, you would feel like part of your life was missing. Using the strength should come relatively effortlessly to you; it shouldn't take a lot of effort trying to action a Signature Strength. Finally, and for us most importantly, the actioning of a Signature Strength should be energising for you and should feel like it is filling your bucket.

Let's see if we can help you identify your Signature Strengths.

> **The truest thing about us is the highest thing about us – not the worst thing – and we should live into that goodness.**
>
> *Charlotte Ostermann*

Exercise 1: Identifying Your Signature Character Strengths

Now it's time to get personal, and for you to think about your Character Strengths. While we all have some awareness of our positive qualities, from experience it is evident that many people are either unaware of, or unable to describe, their own Character Strengths. Let's see if we can help you with this.

Part 1: My intuitive response

Reflecting on your behaviours, how you think of yourself, and how others have described you, you have some awareness of your Character Strengths, and so we invite you to nominate your top-five, based on your intuition.

Below you will find the official list of the twenty-four VIA Character Strengths in alphabetical order. Your task is to select five of these strengths which you feel most strongly describe you as a person at this stage of your life. Please record them below. The formal VIA definition for each Character Strength can be found in Appendix 2.

VIA Character Strengths

- Appreciation of beauty and excellence
- Bravery
- Creativity
- Curiosity
- Fairness
- Forgiveness
- Gratitude
- Honesty
- Hope
- Humility
- Humour
- Judgement
- Kindness
- Leadership
- Love
- Love of learning
- Perseverance
- Perspective
- Prudence
- Self-regulation
- Social intelligence
- Spirituality
- Teamwork
- Zest

My intuitive top-five

- _____
- _____
- _____
- _____
- _____

Part 2: My VIA survey response

The VIA Survey is a free self-assessment that takes around ten minutes to complete. The survey has been translated into more than forty languages and it has now been taken by over twenty million people. On completing the survey, you will be presented with a ranked profile of your strengths. Enjoy gaining valuable self-knowledge from this survey. To complete the survey, visit: www.viacharacter.org/account/register

Having taken the survey, record your Character Strengths profile below:

1 _____   13 _____

2 _____   14 _____

3 _____   15 _____

4 _____   16 _____

5 _____   17 _____

6 _____   18 _____

7 _____   19 _____

8 _____   20 _____

9 _____   21 _____

10 _____   22 _____

11 _____   23 _____

12 _____   24 _____

When I first saw my VIA Character Strengths profile, I literally thought to myself, *I am a legend*! Perseverance was ranked number one, which is very important to me. Fairness, Zest and Kindness were in my top-five, and I thought, *This survey is pretty cool*! I then looked to the bottom of the list; seeing Appreciation of beauty and excellence at number twenty-four. Social intelligence, Humour, and bravery were pretty far down there as well, and I thought, *Maybe I'm not such a legend*!

Having supported thousands of people to identify and explore their strengths profiles, we believe it's healthy and appropriate to get a bit of a lift from seeing your highest Character Strengths. Our strengths help us believe in ourselves and help us believe in others. Your lesser strengths are simply other opportunities and other tools that you now know exist within you and that you can draw upon in certain situations.

Part 3: My current Signature Character Strengths

Remember the three E words that generally apply to Signature Character Strengths?

Essential, **e**ffortless, and **e**nergising.

Now, keeping in mind your intuitive response, your survey results, and the three Es – we would like you to write down your Signature Strengths. Can we suggest at least three and may be no more than eight. Many people find that five is a good number.

For each of your Signature Strengths, we would like you to write one accompanying sentence, either about what the strength means to you, or how important it is to you, or how you and/or others benefit from your use of this strength. An example is provided below.

Example: Humour – I look for the light and funny moments in life and try to bring a sense of playfulness to others in my life.

My current Signature Character Strengths are:

- _____
  _____

- _____
  _____

-

-

-

AWE? (And what else?)

A Word Of Caution

It's important to note that the ranking of strengths is not a personality profile. That's because strengths are within our control to develop if we choose to. If you'd like to exercise more Gratitude in your life, for example, there are a range of evidence-based strategies, such as keeping a gratitude journal, that you can practice to increase your access to and refine that strength.

Strengths Blindness

It is common for people to have a level of strengths awareness; these are the strengths they are already aware of as some of their highest strengths, and are therefore confirmed by the survey. However, it is also common for people to have a level of strengths blindness, where they aren't fully aware of some of their Signature Strengths, and the survey helps them to recognise some of their personal qualities in a different light.

For me personally, I was aware that Perseverance was a quality that was very important to me, and it energised me, but I was equally surprised that Fairness was one of my Signature Strengths. Now, through deeper reflection, I notice how Fairness has guided a wide range of my personal and professional actions for many years.

Exercise 2: My Signature Strengths Stories

To help you truly own your Signature Strengths, it can be helpful to describe a time when you felt you actioned a specific strength in such a way that allowed you to be at your best and contributed to enhancing the wellbeing of yourself and/or others.

We have provided space below for you to write a different story for two of your Signature Strengths. If you would like to do this for more of your strengths, please go right ahead and grab some extra paper.

You may wish to close your eyes and think of the countless times you have actioned this strength, and then hone in on one particular story that brings a smile to your face, where you feel proud of the way you harnessed your Signature Strength.

Signature Strength story for _____

Signature Strength story for _____

AWE?

_____

_____

_____

_____

Note: We invite you to look back over your stories – did you truly embrace your Signature Strength, and/or did you throw in some disclaimers or retractions? It is not always easy to own and acknowledge your strengths, but we hope this exercise helped.

Exercise 3: Growing One Of My Character Strengths

Is there a particular strength you would like to grow? As you look through your Character Strengths profile, is there a strength that possibly lies outside your top-ten that you would like to develop and become more proficient at using?

Let's say, for example, that I would like to grow my Character Strength of Curiosity. My challenge then is to think of ways that I can action my curiosity. This might be at work, with my children, when I meet new people, or as I learn more about a particular hobby or interest.

In a nutshell, if you can find new ways to action a particular strength more frequently across different situations, it makes sense that you will become more adept and familiar with that strength.

There is no doubt you have the capacity to grow a chosen strength.

Character Strength I would like to grow: _____

Use the space provided to respond to the following questions:
- Why do I want to grow this strength?
- How will I go about growing this strength?
- Can one of my existing Signature Strengths help me grow this strength?

Reflections:

Step 1: My Manifesto Draft Response

Having completed the exercises and reflected upon the information within *Step 1: The Energising Step*, it is now time to write your draft response to the key question in this chapter.

What are my Signature Character Strengths?

Note: Please feel free to be expansive with your response, rather than simply listing four or five positive qualities.

My Signature Character Strengths include ...

_____

_____

_____

_____

_____

_____

_____

Step 1: The Energising Step – Case Studies

My Signature Character Strengths include ...

Forgiveness – Allows me to walk through this world with an open heart.

Appreciation of beauty and excellence – Evokes a sense of awe.

Creativity – Allows my mind to grow and flow.

Fairness – Keeps me humble.

Social awareness – Supports my ability for human connection.

My Signature Character Strengths include ...

Honesty – Genuine, sincere, integrity where inside = outside.

Kindness – Small things done with great love.

Judgement – Not jumping to conclusions, not rigid.

Fairness – Treat others how I would like to be treated.

Appreciation of beauty and excellence – Notice the beauty in the everyday.

Humour – Always look on the light side of life.

My Signature Character Strengths include ...

Leadership – I strive to guide people to reach their full potential.

Perseverance – I never give up.

Perspective – I always look at the bigger picture.

Love of learning – I am always looking to learn more.

Appreciation of beauty and excellence – I notice and feel in awe of my surroundings.

My Signature Character Strengths include …

Love of learning – Learning gives me a 'spark' while broadening my world each day.

Perspective – Being able to see and communicate the 'signal in the noise' of life is natural to me but highly valued by others.

Curiosity – Being interested just because I am, and letting curiosity guide me, brings variety and wonder into my daily life.

Creativity – My creativity is more 'incremental improvement' than 'revolutionary' but it is also persistently prevalent.

Honesty – Being genuine and sincere in myself (inwardly and outwardly) is the only way I can be without exhausting my reserves.

Leadership – I am a natural, and therefore often by default, leader, as my sense of perspective makes finding pathways forward easy, so I often seem to step up without even really realising it.

My Signature Character Strengths include …

Humour – Through living playfully.

Love of learning – Because I love seeking knowledge.

Honesty – I express it through how I nurture my relationships.

Creativity – Enables me to problem solve and be excited by challenges.

Judgement – I use this strength in critically evaluating options and making decisions I am confident in.

My Signature Character Strengths include …

Forgiveness, Fairness, Curiosity, Kindness, Perspective.

My forgiveness reflection: I sacked a staff member for not being willing to work with another staff member after giving them a number of opportunities. When asked in a job interview how I could have handled that differently, I said I would have sacked them quickly rather than letting it drag on. On reflection, I wish I had said I would have put more effort into resolving the situation and found a way not to sack them.

My curiosity reflection: I am learning in many personal situations that curiosity is the opposite of defensiveness and leads to much better interactions.

My Signature Character Strengths are more 'mild-mannered reporter' than 'superman'. Gentle powers, I hope.

7 The Contribution Step

6 The Connection Step

5 The Releasing Step

4 The Visionary Step

3 The Mattering Step

2 The Courageous Step

1 The Energising Step

Chapter 8:
Step 2: The Courageous Step

Justin

Your beliefs become your thoughts, Your thoughts become your words, Your words become your actions, Your actions become your habits, Your habits become your **values**, Your **values** become your destiny.

Mahatma Gandhi

As you place your energised foot firmly on our second step, we invite you to reflect upon something you did this morning. Can you think of one thing in particular that resonates with you and stands out as important?

Maybe it was a fitness activity, maybe it was a conversation with a loved one, maybe it was reading or watching the news. Now that you have thought of something, we would like you to ask yourself, 'Which core value(s) underpinned my decision to carry out that particular activity this morning?' Maybe it was your core value of living a healthy life, maybe it was your love of family, or your value of being informed and up to date.

Most likely you hadn't consciously realised or appreciated the core value that was driving your action this morning, but we suggest there definitely was one. Can you now consider if the action that you are reflecting upon is an action that you repeat on several or many mornings each week? If it is, then your action has become a habit, and as Gandhi succinctly expresses, these regular habits will become your values, which will in turn shape your destiny.

Once you begin looking for core values, you begin to see them in many of your interactions, decisions, and behaviours across the course of your day.

What Are Values?

Dr Russ Harris describes values as 'your heart's deepest desires for how you want to be as a human being'. Your values can become, or already are, your compass. They give you direction in your life – the direction you wish to head in.

It is possible to have unhealthy or destructive values that are harmful to yourself or others. However, unsurprisingly, our focus within this chapter is toward *healthy* and *constructive* values that treat the self and others with dignity, compassion, and respect. Healthy values help us to connect with a zoomed-out view of our lives, because they orient us to what is good for us in the long run. When you think about your personal values, consider how you want to behave, how you want to interact with others, and how you want to live your life.

It is important to acknowledge that we are shaped by our life experiences, by our social worlds, how our families raised us, and the cultures and communities of which we have been a part. Over time, we adopt and then adapt the values and norms held by these various social groups, making them our own and hence shaping our identity. As you consider and articulate your core values, you may like to reflect upon the significant influences and experiences in your life to date.

How Do Values Differ From Strengths And Goals?

Remember that Character Strengths are universal, positive human qualities. Therefore, all Character Strengths can be categorised as values – your heart's deepest desires. But if your values represent what you aspire to, then your Signature Character Strengths encapsulate who you currently are, and how you commonly act.

It is normal for there to be overlap in values and Signature Character Strengths. In our comprehensive table of values in Exercise 1, all twenty-four Character Strengths are represented – sixteen exactly – and eight through synonyms. In the table, you will also find terms such as 'success', 'travel' and 'financial stability'. These are all common desires, but are not classifiable as Character Strengths.

Furthermore, values tend to be much less specific than goals. Values are not a place a person arrives at like goals – rather, values are guiding principles that provide a foundation and rationale for our goals.

Secondly, values tend to be explicitly prosocial. They directly benefit the community as well as the individual. The knowledge that your values will contribute to your community and also influence the lives of your family and friends can add an extra layer of significance to this work. It's not to say that goals can't be of benefit to others, but that goals tend to mostly benefit the individual. Would you agree?

And thirdly, values, unlike goals, are rarely actually achieved. There is no finish line for our values – this is what constitutes their stability over time. As we can never actually achieve or tick off our values; they tend to stay with us, often forever.

However, like your goals, you still get to choose your values, and it is possible for you to add, soften, or change your values from time to time. And, for you, now is the time to courageously consider and then articulate the core values that will act as your compass at this time in your life!

The Courageous Question

What do I stand for?

What: We want to be able to name specific values. We provide you with an extensive list to help you respond to this question.

I: This is not the time to be thinking of others and what they stand for – it is all about you. Take this time to immerse yourself in you and your values.

Stand for: What will you accept or tolerate, and what will you not accept or tolerate? A bystander stands by and watches and accepts the situation. An upstander stands up for what they believe is right, appropriate, and acceptable. As you consider your core values – the qualities that represent you, how you want to behave, and how you want to live your life – know that these are not just nice qualities; they are deeply held values that you are willing to stand up for!

Exercise 1: Connecting To My Core Values

It's time to connect to what is really important to you, what you stand for, and how you want to relate to the world. We would love to help you truly know and articulate your core values.

We refer to 'core values' as the values that are most central, most important, most deeply valued by you.

Interestingly, despite how important and impactful they are, it is not particularly common in our society for people to talk about values very much. We suspect you can't think of a time when a friend directly asked you, 'Tell us about your core values?' While it is common for someone to ask, 'How's work going?', I haven't (yet) had anyone ask me, 'How are your core values going?'

On the following page you will find a list of 150 values regarded by most societies as important. We would like you to whittle this list down to the five of the most important values to you – your core values!

- If this feels an almost impossible task to you, you are correct! The following reflection questions may help you as you move through the three steps below.
- Could you live a full and meaningful life without this value?
- Would this value still be important if no-one knew you actioned it?
- Is this value an important part of who you want to be?
- Does this value motivate you to act?

Phase 1: Very important to *you*.

With a pen in hand, read through the list of 150 values and simply place a tick beside ones that intuitively feel very important to you. Remember, that all of them are important values, but in this first pass we are looking for ones which are very important to you. Maybe aim to tick around twenty to thirty of the values on the list.

Phase 2: Very, very important to *you*.

Now, just looking at the short-list of values you have ticked, which ones of these are very, very important to you? Place a second tick on around ten of the values on your list.

Phase 3: Very, very, very important to *you*.

Can you put a third tick on only five of the values? It is helpful and empowering to have a small, manageable list of core values that truly represent your heart's deepest desires for how you want to be as a human being.

(Of course, in reality, you will have far more than five values that direct your life, but knowing and articulating five core values is your goal in this exercise.)

Phase 4: Record your top-five core *values*.

- _____

- _____

- _____

- _____

A List Of 150 Courageous Values

Acceptance	Courage	Happiness	Mindfulness	Self-respect
Accountability	Creativity	Harmony	Openness	Serenity
Achievement	Curiosity	Health	Optimism	Sexuality
Adaptability	Determination	Home	Order	Service
Adventure	Dignity	Honesty	Parenting	Simplicity
Altruism	Diversity	Hope	Patience	Spirituality
Ambition	Efficiency	Humility	Patriotism	Sportsmanship
Assertiveness	Environment	Intimacy	Peace	Stability
Authenticity	Equality	Humour	Perseverance	Status
Authority	Ethics	Inclusion	Personal fulfillment	Stewardship
Autonomy	Excellence	Independence	Pleasure	Success
Balance	Excitement	Influence	Poise	Teamwork
Beauty	Fairness	Initiative	Popularity	Thrift
Being the best	Flexibility	Inner Harmony	Power	Time
Belonging	Faith	Integrity	Pride	Tradition
Boldness	Fame	Intuition	Recognition	Travel
Career	Family	Job security	Reliability	Trust
Caring	Financial stability	Joy	Religion	Trustworthiness
Challenge	Forgiveness	Justice	Reputation	Truth
Citizenship	Freedom	Kindness	Resourcefulness	Understanding
Collaboration	Friendship	Knowledge	Reciprocity	Uniqueness
Commitment	Friendships	Leadership	Respect	Usefulness
Community	Fitness	Learning	Romance	Vision
Compassion	Fun	Legacy	Responsibility	Vulnerability
Competence	Future generations	Leisure	Risk-taking	Wealth
Confidence	Generosity	Love	Safety	Wellbeing
Connection	Giving back	Loyalty	Security	Wholeheartedness
Contentment	Grace	Making a difference	Self-discipline	Wisdom
Contribution	Gratitude	Meaningful work	Self-expression	*Write your own:*
Cooperation	Growth	Nature	Self-care	

Instead of thinking what will others think of me if I say or do that, I started to think what will I think of myself if I don't say or do that.

Anon

Exercise 2: Core Values Check-In

Living with integrity implies soundness of moral character, but even more importantly it refers to a state of being fully integrated – of being whole, entire, or undivided. In reality this means living a life where your thoughts, words, and actions are integrated and aligned with your core values.

So firstly, you must articulate your values – tick! Now we invite you to check in on these five values and write down one example of how this value has motivated you to act in the past, and also to record an opportunity for how you might integrate this value into your future life.

1. My core value of _____

An example of how this value has motivated me to act in the past is …

_____

_____

A future opportunity for how I can integrate this value into my life is …

_____

_____

2. My core value of _____

An example of how this value has motivated me to act in the past is …

_____

_____

A future opportunity for how I can integrate this value into my life is …

_____

_____

3. My core value of _____

An example of how this value has motivated me to act in the past is …

_____

_____

A future opportunity for how I can integrate this value into my life is…

_____

_____

4. My core value of _____

An example of how this value has motivated me to act in the past is ...

_____

_____

A future opportunity for how I can integrate this value into my life is ...

_____

_____

5. My core value of _____

An example of how this value has motivated me to act in the past is ...

_____

_____

A future opportunity for how I can integrate this value into my life is ...

_____

_____

AWE? (And what else?) ...

And what else are you thinking about as you reflect deeply on your core values?

_____

_____

_____

_____

Asking AWE two times gives you more options, and maybe even better options now that you have started your thinking.

Exercise 3: Values I Admire

Think of a person in your life who you deeply admire and respect. What values do you admire in them? How do they bring those values into their life?

Record your reflections below.

We trust you enjoyed the above exercise. Quite possibly the hardest part was choosing just one person to reflect upon. Of course, you are most welcome to select more individuals and repeat this exercise at any time in the future.

Now, having pared down a list of 150 values to your five core values, and having described how you hope to integrate such values, it is time to respond to the question: 'What do I stand for?'

Like many of the key questions across these seven steps, your responses may be stable over time, or they might be dynamic and changing, due to 'where you are at'.

In my twenties, I wore a necklace that had lettered dice on it, spelling out 'C.H.E.E.R.S'. It was a word I enjoyed saying to friends and families; I was known for saying 'cheers' when I was leaving, or 'cheers' when I was expressing my thanks. But more importantly, I designed this necklace around a mantra of my core values at the time: it stood for Confidence, Honesty, Enthusiasm, Excellence, Respect, and Smile.

Now that I'm in my fifties, my core values are different, spelling out 'C.C.C.W.E': Caring, Contribution, Challenge, Wisdom, and Excitement. I prioritise caring for others; I enjoy challenging myself; I aim to make a lasting contribution (in the field of wellbeing education); I treasure gaining in wisdom; and I welcome living an exciting life. I also have key goals and projects that I am pursuing under each of these values. This book is a current key project under Contribution.

As you draft your responses to this step, feel free in the knowledge that the core values you list are those which feel the most relevant and important to you at this time in your life.

Step 2: My Manifesto Draft Response

Having completed the exercises and reflected upon the information within *Step 2: The Courageous Step*, it is now time to write your draft response to the key question in this chapter.

What do I stand for?

I stand for ...

When your values are clear to you, making decisions becomes easier, and living courageously becomes easier.

Step 2: The Courageous Step – Case Studies

I stand for ...

Creating a life for myself that is full of excitement, where I seek and take the time to appreciate all the things in everyday life that bring joy, whether in big or small ways.

I also stand for injecting humour into otherwise mundane or difficult circumstances wherever possible and to offer laughter and playfulness to other peoples' lives.

I also stand for living a creative life, whether it is through my work or as a hobby, and to inspire others to do the same. I would also like to foster a sense of belonging in the spaces and communities I create, lead and share with others, and to support and empower people from all walks of life to feel safe to express themselves and be heard when they do.

I stand for ...

The dignity of all humans. I believe all should have access to basic fundamental human rights. I believe we should celebrate the wonderful diversity that exists throughout humanity, accepting this diversity through education, personal discovery, engaging with peoples from diverse backgrounds, and listening and gently encouraging those who do not share these values to consider other points of view. Despite the great diversity which exists across the globe, by accepting others, I believe we will come to realise how similar we all are.

I stand for ...

Family. I have always had this value in the past by helping out my grandpa in palliative care on night shifts and in the future I will integrate this value at family gatherings by being more assertive in mingling.

I stand for caring. I have used this value in the past by caring for my dog and all his needs and in the future I will integrate this value in my work as a nurse.

I stand for integrity. I have used this value in the past by standing up for my peers when they were being bullied and in the future I will integrate this value by advocating for my patients and other people I come across in life as needed.

I stand for ...

Being an authentic, grounded person who can be loved, and can express love. I value wellbeing and I am motivated to prioritise my own wellbeing, and also to empower others to strengthen their wellbeing. I have a strong desire to be of service to others and to make a positive contribution to the world which will make a difference now and for future generations.

I stand for ...

Joy, friendship, excellence, pride, and poise.

I value being happy and feeling joy in my life to be of high importance. I hold my friendships very close to my heart. I value achieving excellence in everything I do and aim to be proud of my actions in doing so. I also value having the confidence, wisdom, and kindness to carry and conduct myself with poise.

7 The Contribution Step

6 The Connection Step

5 The Releasing Step

4 The Visionary Step

3 The Mattering Step

2 The Courageous Step

1 The Energising Step

Chapter 9:
Step 3: The Mattering Step

Sue

The simple act of caring is heroic.

Edward Albert

You have arrived at *Step 3: The Mattering Step*. You are now able to articulate your energising Signature Strengths and have courageously expressed your core values. You are uncovering your authentic self, and now we invite you to explore all things that matter to you, the things that are important to you, that you deeply care about. This step is intentionally deeply personal, deeply subjective, unfiltered, uninhibited, and raw. Silence your inner critic! Let's find out what matters to you.

The Mattering Question

'What do I care deeply about?'

Your enjoyable challenge is to list the essential things which matter at the core of your unique self. You are probably thinking this is way too general and too hard and too impossible of a question to even begin! Well, let's give you a way in by breaking it up into three themes. The themes we suggest are Personal, Others, and World, which we playfully refer to as: POW!

Personal: Includes your wellbeing, health, leisure, interests, beliefs.

Others: Includes family, friends, work, community, society.

World: Includes humankind, the environment, our planet and universe.

A key factor is ... passion!

Don't even bother writing down things you feel lukewarm about, or even worse, that you feel you *should* care about! This is *your* list, and you don't need to show it to anyone else if you don't want to. The *shoulds* are those expectations which come from the tapes in your head – the voices, people, and beliefs from others, both past and present. Recognise them as potential blockers or self-limiters and override them if you don't want to choose them! (More about blockers and self-limiters in *Step 5: The Releasing Step*.) So, write down the things – including the people – that *you* feel passionately about. We have mentioned this before, but let me say it again here: there is *no rush* with this process.

What do I care deeply about?

What: These are things, not reasons. All the things you can think of without second-guessing, rationalising, justifying. List them.

I: This is about you, no-one else, no matter how much you love, admire, respect, or are obligated to them. It is your unique life you are concerned with.

Deeply: These lie at your core. They are at the level of your values and beliefs. They are essential to you.

Care: This is one of those all-encompassing words on the love continuum. Care encapsulates 'mattering'. These are the things that make you, you, and without which you are not you.

If you have lived this much of your life without consciously constructing this list or reflecting in this way, then you do not have to churn it out in five minutes! Take the time you need as you think on and gradually add to this list of things. Go about your day with the question in your mind, and if something occurs to you, jot it down.

It may be time-specific

When you are thinking of what you care deeply about, some of the things or the people may be specific to this moment in time while others may be life-long. In the spirit of starting where you are at (introduced and explored in *Starting Where You Are At*), focus on who and what matters *now*.

Alright, so you know you need to think about what you care deeply about, and perhaps you have some ideas rushing around your head, but you're still not really sure if you are on the right track! Trust me, I know the feeling. You may feel some fear creeping in – concerns that you might not be a very deep thinker and what you come up with might not cut the mustard. But have a go! Be prepared to surprise yourself! You have already done amazing work in *Steps 1* and *2*. You are on a roll now!

Exercise 1: POW Cares!

As this is your first run-through, don't be overly fussed about polishing your words – yet! Just write your responses in bullet points as they come to you and leave the refining work for later.

Personal cares – What do I care deeply about?

- _____

- _____

- _____

- _____

This includes things which matter to you personally, such as wellbeing, health, leisure and interests, and beliefs.

Now that you have got your thinking started, is there anything else you might add?

AWE? (And what else?)

- _____

- _____

Others cares – What do I care deeply about?

- _____

- _____

- _____

This includes family, friends, work, community, and society.

AWE?

- _____

- _____

World cares – What do I care deeply about?

- _____

- _____

- _____

This includes humankind, the environment, our planet and universe.

AWE?

- _____

- _____

Exercise 2: What Impresses Me?

When I am thinking about other people and what impresses me about them, I would have to say integrity: a sense that they are living their lives in complete congruence. As I say this, Sister Brigid Arthur, a Brigidine nun who was the principal of the secondary school I attended as a teenager, comes to mind. I think it is fair to say that my own sense of fairness, justice and equity are derived from this woman.

A small example of Sister Brigid in action might help you picture her. She was in her first principalship when I was a student, and this story comes from a period of many years since, but I just loved it when I heard it. As principal, she was conducting interviews for teaching positions in the school, seeking to appoint a secondary school music teacher.

The candidate she was interviewing was tired of being inauthentic in their career prospects, and told her, 'I just want you to know that I am gay.' Sister Brigid's response was, 'Okay, but can you teach music?' This was in the 1980s!

I love the perspective she showed here – the fairness, and the humour! What a combination!

I would like you to think now of a particular person you know, or know of, who impresses you. Alternatively, write about the kinds of qualities in a person who impress you.

I am impressed by ...

Exercise 3: When Did I Last Experience ...

Let us introduce another method of uncovering the things you care most deeply about by tapping into powerful emotions that all human beings experience.

Below, we have provided a list of ten key positive emotions and invite you to describe a time when you recently experienced each of them. No need to think too hard about this; just write down what first comes to mind. You will find a brief descriptor of each of the ten emotions in Appendix 3.

I surprised myself when I thought about this list, considering recent examples of how each of the emotions have shown up in my life, when *contentment* came up. Really? Yes! As I am writing this book with Justin, and as I am contemplating the next workshop for **my manifesto**, I realise that this work is what I have been preparing for my whole life! I am content. It may sound twee, but until I had 'grown up' I wasn't able to just stop and 'be'. (Of course, when I say, 'grown up', I mean my inner age, not my chronological one!) And of course, this state of contentment is not static – as we can't hold on to emotional states – but I do know it now and will know it again.

I would like you now to take each of these emotions in turn and write an example of when you last experienced them in your life. I hope this brings you joy.

I last experienced ...

Positive emotion	Describe a time when you recently experienced this positive emotion
Joy	
Gratitude	
Contentment	
Curiosity	
Hope	
Pride	
Amusement	
Inspiration	
Awe	
Love	

Reflection

Having completed this exercise, we invite you to write a reflection on what this uncovered for you. Did it raise any other deep cares?

_____

_____

_____

_____

AWE?

_____

_____

_____

_____

Intentionally, we haven't asked you to complete this exercise for ten common negative emotions, but we acknowledge that this can be another very powerful exercise and can also result in uncovering deep cares.

Generating Positive Emotions

We all understand that emotions can arise due to something external that is beyond our control. For example, from a positive emotional perspective, you might feel grateful when a colleague makes you a cup of tea, or hopeful when they offer to help you with a particular project, or amused when they share a funny story. In each of these situations, the positive emotions are experienced internally due to a kind external action from a colleague. This is great, but it is also out of our control.

Having completed this exercise, you can probably recognise occasions where your emotional experience was due to the actions of others or your environment. However, even more importantly, we hope that you can recognise times when you initiated thoughts or actions that generated positive emotions.

It is powerful to appreciate that you can intentionally generate different positive emotions. You may use music to generate inspiration; you may go for a walk in nature to trigger contentment; you may think in a particular way to elicit gratitude; you may watch a particular TV series to initiate amusement; you may prioritise a particular conversation or activity to spark joy or awe. Yes, emotions can happen to us, and yes, we can also *make* emotions happen! As you arrive home, or arrive at work, can you think of an emotional state you would like to experience and/or spark in others?

So, as you prepare to provide your response to what you deeply care about, understand that you often have more power than you think over generating positive emotions and thereby supporting and contributing to your deepest cares.

Step 3: My Manifesto Draft Response

Having completed the exercises and reflected upon the information within *Step 3: The Mattering Step*, it is now time to write your draft response to the key question in this chapter.

What do I care deeply about?

I care deeply about ...

Step 3: The Mattering Step – Case Studies

I care deeply about …

My two beautiful children; my wishes for them, today and in the future, are all encompassing and infinite. I deeply care about my husband and the health of our relationship and our unconditional love. I deeply care about my parents and their ability to age long and well. I deeply care about my closest friends, their trials and tribulations. And I deeply care about myself too; my dreams, my health, my wellbeing and contentment in life. May I forever be strong, content and able to find pleasure in life … and in dark chocolate!

I care deeply about …

Maintaining good self-care practices for myself daily and taking the time to look after my mental and physical wellbeing, because I know it enables me to show up as my best self. I care about incorporating creativity into my everyday life, and having creative practices where I am able to express myself and produce new work. I care deeply about inspiring and empowering others to express themselves creatively. I care deeply about being able to feel safe in all my relationships. I care deeply about my close family and friends and the wellbeing of the people who are important in my life. I care deeply about having a career and life I am passionate about, and hobbies which excite my soul. I care deeply about travelling and having new experiences. I care deeply about all people around the world having access to safety and shelter. I care deeply about fairness and equality for all beings. Right now, I care deeply about creating structure in my life, and being disciplined about getting my work done.

I care deeply about ...

- Connection and creation.
- Intentional connection and gratitude for those I love.
- Creation of methodical systems to achieve goals.
- Seeking kindred spirits.
- Smiling.
- Standing barefoot in the grass.
- Swimming in the ocean.

I care deeply about ...

- My commitment to self.
- My commitment to relationships.
- My commitment to community.

I care deeply about ...

Creating a safe space for people to feel they can be themselves and express themselves. Maintaining my peace through connection with nature, play, creativity, and people. Nourishing myself and my loved ones through food, laughter, play, and love.

I care deeply about ...

My own wellbeing. I care deeply about those closest to me. I care about those who struggle with life. I care deeply about our local communities. I care about Australia. I care about the global issues which threaten our very existence. I care about the inequalities that exist on a local, regional, and global scale.

I also believe that in order to manage such thoughts, we need to look after our immediate selves and those we interact with, whether they are family, friends, colleagues, the people we meet in our day-to-day existence, or complete strangers. I believe that we are capable of changing our mindsets so that we can seek the positive: we can create environments that give us happiness; we can be kind to people; we can give and expect nothing in return.

We can think global by acting local. Small things matter. Small acts of kindness matter. Forgiving those who have done you some harm matters. Giving to those in need – be it through labour, charities, actions or money – matters. You feel good giving, while those who receive benefit. A win-win situation.

I care deeply about the messages we receive via social media, mainstream media, and the dark web. I care about the impact negative reporting might have on the psyche of an individual, family, group, or country. I believe there is more good in this world – there are far more acts of kindness than acts of aggression. Alas, one act of violence can destroy so much of the good that has accumulated. Thus, I go back to the need for acceptance, for gratitude, a sense of belonging, and treating all with dignity.

7 The Contribution Step

6 The Connection Step

5 The Releasing Step

4 The Visionary Step

3 The Mattering Step

2 The Courageous Step

1 The Energising Step

Chapter 10:
Step 4: The Visionary Step

Sue

**You may say I'm a dreamer,
but I'm not the only one ...**

John Lennon

I get a shiver up my spine when I see the word 'visionary'. It is only in recent times that I have even allowed myself to think that I could claim that word for myself. You see, as a child, my Mum called me a dreamer – 'There goes Suzi, head in the clouds and nose in a book.' While this might be interpreted only on the mild side of criticism, it nevertheless sounded like a cutting criticism to my young self. However, recently I've come across a positive reconstruction of 'dreamer' when a synonym was offered: visionary. I could have cried for joy. Immediately I saw myself differently.

So for you: with my permission, approach the visionary question with excitement and invite your inner child to dream. And as you know, we are not the only ones.

The Visionary Question

'What do I dream about?'

When I started to write blogs for the **my manifesto** web page, after I finished my classroom English teaching, I found the going tough and the progress slow. I had all sorts of expectations in my head, like, *You're an English teacher, you should be good at writing*, and, *You're an avid reader*, and, *You're an Honours graduate* – all of which made my attempts painful indeed. Until Justin said to me, 'Sue, just be playful with it.'

That was a revelatory suggestion for me. *You* know that I am earnest; *you* know that I have trouble with being 'enough', and *you* know I am a dreamer.

I know that Humour and Playfulness are among the twenty-four Character Strengths of which Justin writes so beautifully and authoritatively in *Step 1: The Energising Step* of this book. Could I allow myself to have this element of lightness in my life, too?

Well, the result of this approach is evident as we near one hundred blogs that Justin and I have subsequently written, not to mention this book! I therefore now give you permission to be playful with this question and indeed all of the work suggested in this book! Don't get me wrong – it doesn't mean that you should be insincere or ingenuine. It just means that you do not need to sabotage yourself. Write freely and compassionately.

What do I dream about?

What: As always with a 'what' question, you are invited to think of all the possibilities without second-guessing yourself.

I: This is the time to be subjective – deeply so. It is not about anyone else, and the only expectations to place on yourself are yours.

Dream: This word may be problematic for some of you. It does not have to be literal* – the dreams you have while you are asleep – but rather a figurative expression. In this sense, it is your wishes, imaginings, hopes, aspirations for yourself, and perhaps the world.

Note: Many people keep dream diaries and if this is your practice and you find it helpful for capturing what your subconscious may be telling you, then by all means use this term literally and figuratively.

Exercise 1: POW Dreams!

We invite you to target each of the POW! themes as you identify your dream elements and build them from your imagination.

Personal: Includes your wellbeing, health, leisure, interests, beliefs.

Others: Includes family, friends, work, community, society.

World: Includes humankind, the environment, our planet and universe.

If you find it too hard to free yourself from your current reality when thinking of your dreams for your life, try moving ahead in time (say two, three, five, or however many years) to see if this releases you.

Personal: My dreams for myself – What arises for me?

- _____

- _____

- _____

- _____

Regularly asking yourself the helpful inspiring AWE question gives you more options – maybe even better options.

AWE? (And what else?)

- _____

- _____

Others: My dreams for others – What arises for me?

- _____
- _____
- _____
- _____

AWE?

- _____
- _____

World: My dreams for our world – What arises for me?

- _____
- _____
- _____
- _____

AWE?

- _____
- _____

Exercise 2: Another Angle

What does my version of excellence and success look like?
This question may suit you better, particularly if you are doing this exercise with a work focus. Sometimes, if this is your intention, 'dreams' may not resonate with you. Similarly, you may choose excellence or success or a combination of both as your preferred terms. It is all about what works for you. Notice it is also *your* version, with the implicit understanding that everyone has their own benchmarks for excellence and success.

'What does my version of excellence and success look like?'

Personal – What does my version of excellence and success look like in me?

- _____

- _____

- _____

- _____

Others – What does my version of excellence and success look like in others?

- _____
- _____
- _____
- _____

World – What does my version of excellence and success look like in our world?

- _____
- _____
- _____
- _____

Oftentimes when we are living our lives, when we feel most on track, we notice things around us that seem to support us. This is not a new phenomenon; it has been labelled 'synchronicity', and I have seen it attributed to Carl Jung's teachings, though it has many followers. It is a practice of mine to keep a synchronicity journal, as I intentionally look for signs – small ticks of approval – from the world around me. I feel affirmed when I notice it happening. I can also reward myself for these ticks with small or big acts of self-compassion as visible signs that I am living my life well.

You might like to look for ticks and note down what you see in the next day or two. Remember, meaning is what you make of it. Life does not have an objective meaning or order – beyond that of the natural order of the seasons. (Daylight savings debunked my naive view of time! Another human construct!)

Reflection

- _____

- _____

- _____

- _____

- _____

Exercise 3: How Did You Do That?

It is rare when thinking about what we dream about and what we might hope for, to come up with something entirely unrelated to your current reality. However, what you dream about may well be a magnification of an aspect of your life that you wouldn't ordinarily allow yourself to give much airplay, but here is the time and place to go there! I am sticking my neck out by suggesting that all our dreams have some link to our current life *and* that in fact, all the dreams you have listed in Exercise 1 have some link to your life already!

Exercise 1 invited you to identify what your dreams are in the many contexts of your life. Exercise 2 broadened into viewing dreams in an alternate way, such as in excellence or success. Exercise 3 invites you to hone in on those times in your past when you may have caught glimpses of aspects of your dreams, or your success story, being touched on.

For this exercise, let's consider using the blanket term 'vision' for your version of your dreams, or your ideas for what excellence and success looks like.

Ask yourself this question: **When in my life have I seen a glimpse of my vision?**

Describe that time in as much detail as you can. Spend time with it.

_____

_____

_____

_____

Having focused on that time, ask yourself with genuine curiosity:

How did I do that?

_____

_____

_____

_____

Spend time spotting the way this came to pass. Was it because you were using one of your Character Strengths? Can you see one or more of your core values in play? Is it an aspect of your POW cares? Really dig deep here. If you were able to see a dream or success story even only minutely realised, *and* you are able to identify the reason, *and* it was because you were using a Character Strength, or tapping into a core value, or doing something you really care deeply about – *then* you can do it again. You can even add, expand, and grow that little glimpse into something big.

> To accomplish great things, we must not only act, **but also dream**; not only plan, **but also believe.**
>
> **Anatole France**

Step 4: My Manifesto Draft Response

Having completed the exercises and reflected upon the information within *Step 4: The Visionary Step,* it is now time to write your draft response to the key question in this chapter.

What do I dream about?

I dream about ...

Step 4: The Visionary Step – Case Studies

I dream about …

The day I celebrate my hundredth birthday and look back on my life. I feel content and proud as I watch my grown children happy, having achieved or achieving their dreams. I am old, but I still hold the hand of my best friend and life partner and we still manage to make each other laugh. My body is strong and I look out towards my garden full of the vegetables I've grown; I smell a plate of food full of wholefoods from my table; and I reminisce about the successful business I ran while younger. These things I dream of and they make me smile.

I dream about …

- An extraordinary ordinary life.
- Being 'in the position to take the next step'.
- Having a light heart.
- Rich relationships.
- Travelling.
- Meaningful work.
- Caring for people.
- Caring for the world.

I dream about …

Being a healthy happy person who has great wellbeing and is physically strong and fit. I dream about being close with friends and family, who will support me in a successful career. I dream about living on a healthy planet with kind humans.

I dream about ...

A creative space that I have and can express my ideas in.

I dream about my husband, kids, family, and loved ones being comfortable and secure in themselves.

I dream about being confident and secure in myself.

I dream about being comfortable with feeling joy.

I dream about ...

Meaningfully engaging in the twilight years of my life on earth. I dream about the planet I love being cared for so that my children's children's children, and my sister's, brothers', nieces', and nephews' children's children's children will also be able to immerse themselves in the beauties and wonders of planet earth. I dream about the world becoming a kinder and more peaceful place; a place where humanity's vibrant diversity continues to flourish due to the courageous, brave, inspirational leadership found in all walks of life. I dream that existing socio-economic inequalities, in all their forms, can be or are being reduced by local, regional, and global organisations through the lens of authentic cooperation. I dream about each individual being respected and cared for no matter their identity. I also dream about each individual respecting and caring for the communities and groups they belong to. I dream that each community or group or nation accepts all others. I dream that many important future decisions will be owned by the people – no matter the scale of the decision.

I dream.

7 The Contribution Step

6 The Connection Step

5 The Releasing Step

4 The Visionary Step

3 The Mattering Step

2 The Courageous Step

1 The Energising Step

Chapter 11:
Step 5: The Releasing Step

Sue

Often what keeps you from creative living is your self-doubt, your self-judgement, your crushing sense of self-protection.

Elizabeth Gilbert

It might seem odd to be opening a chapter called *The Releasing Step* and to proceed to talk about imperfections, suffering, and limitations. Wow, there should be a big 'BEWARE' heading here. But you might have heard, as we certainly have, of the wellbeing field and positive psychology being referred to as 'happiology'. Well, we don't accept that description or the underlying judgement at all. We want you to know that you, your whole self, is welcome to do this work. And that means all of your imperfections and perceived limitations.

In *Part 1*, we invited you to 'start where you are at'. We are sincere in wanting you to take a 'warts and all' approach to this journey. You are only too aware of your imperfections given we all carry the evolutionary-geared negativity bias. We are not suggesting that you are only welcome in the best version of yourself. Chances are you don't know what that is yet, and finding that out is the point of the journey!

But, we are now ready to acknowledge that we all face challenges. As coaches who use a solutions-focused approach, let's be brave and use the word 'problems' – something that shakes our resolve and ability to live authentically. Some of these problems will be internal – the voices of the many people and influences we have experienced since childhood – and others come from the random events and situations that life serves up. You can't change these problems, but as the wonderful Viktor E. Frankl attests in *Man's Search for Meaning*, you can choose your attitude towards them. A final necessary step, too, is accepting the problems which are out of your control.

My young self, growing up in Broken Hill in the 1950s, bought into the Hollywood fantasy: that there is a 'happy ever after' life which, for whatever reason, was just out of my reach. Somehow, someday,

I would work out the riddle of life and live in that idyllic dream land. Denial, self-sabotage, and constant searching became my ways of being as I came up against my own shortcomings and the unfairness and injustices of life.

Now, in my seventies, I know that I am imperfect *and* I am unique. I also know that life will offer moments of brilliance *and* moments of suffering. Instead of denying or fighting the parts of me that challenge me – my *problems* – I am learning to accept all of me. I am also more prepared for what life serves up: I have my personal manifesto, my guide for who I am and what I stand for, with which I calibrate the decisions I need to make to negotiate the inevitable and random hurdles of life. I am inviting you to love and accept all of yourself and prepare yourself with your guide for life's journey.

The Releasing Question

What can I release myself from?

What: All the things you can think of.

Can: Able to, within my power.

Release: Let go; liberate.

From: Problems, difficulties, stumbling blocks, obstacles.

You will notice I made the choice of 'liberating' for releasing because the connotations have so much PEA (Positive Energy Attraction) for me and, I hope, for you. Oh, to be liberated from the things that agitate us and cause us to stumble. Of course, sometimes we might just have to work through them, or even accept them if they are beyond our control.

Let's begin to explore and uncover what we need to release ourselves from. In Exercise 1, we ask you to name the problem, those self-limiting beliefs, and then practise releasing yourself. In Exercise 2, we invite you to flip the problem, the problems outside of your control, by changing your attitude. In Exercise 3, we suggest you use The Miracle Question (a wonderful Solution Focus tool) to imagine the problem vanished and notice the releasing effect on your behaviour.

Exercise 1: Naming The Problem

Coaches know that if you can 'name the problem' – the thing that is blocking you – and pin it down, this is the starting point to being able to manage it. No matter what the external reality might be, many of our problems have their own energy. We'll call these 'limiting beliefs': those hard-to-shake beliefs which threaten to take us down the moment we step outside our comfort zone.

Let's start with the problems that are near to home and of our own making!

Before I ask you to do something that I wouldn't do myself, I will let you in on one of my **self-limiting beliefs**: I am not a risk-taker; I play it safe. But, when I did the exercise below about my self-*supporting* beliefs, I placed on the list, 'I go first!', and, 'I say "Yes to life!"' Seems a bit contradictory, doesn't it? Go on, laugh! You have my permission.

Taking a moment to reflect on both my self-supporting statements, I realised they are deliberate strategies chosen precisely because I know I have the tendency to hide and stay safe. I may not be able to rid myself of these self-limiting tendencies – because I recognise their roots in my childhood fears – but I can manage them by adopting specific self-supporting tools to ensure they do not immobilise me.

Self-limiting beliefs

Part 1: My self-limiting beliefs

Write down any self-limiting beliefs that you have about yourself. I would like to encourage you by sharing some of mine.

- I am not a risk-taker.
- I am not a good enough writer.
- I am intellectually no giant.
- I am self-absorbed.
- I am no fun to be with.

That is enough! My cheeks are burning.

Your turn
Part 1: My self-limiting beliefs

- I am _____
- I am _____
- I am _____
- I am _____
- I am _____
- I am _____

Part 2: My self-supporting beliefs

These are all the positives that you know (really, you do) about yourself and your capabilities. They are yours alone to see. Don't hide from yourself what you are probably – like me – an expert at hiding from (or admitting to) others. By the way, there is no scarcity paradigm here: you declaring yourself capable of something does not prevent someone else from being capable of it, too! It is also not a competition. Be in integrity as you attest to your skills and attributes.

Here are some of mine to start you off:
- I am loving.
- I am resourceful.
- I am spiritually alive.
- I am compassionate.
- I am human.

Your turn
Part 2: My self-supporting beliefs

- I am _____

- I am _____

- I am _____

- I am _____

- I am _____

- I am _____

Part 3: Let's see these lists side by side

We invite you to compare the lists and spot the contradictions! How can you be both? In believing the self-supporting list, we encourage you to rip, throw out, or burn the self-limiting beliefs list (be careful to remove it from the book first!). This ceremony makes the point that we are all holding ourselves back with the language we adopt about ourselves, despite the in-your-face absurdity and contradictions of much of it! What this language does is stop us in our tracks; immobilises us. To meet our problems, it is essential we release ourselves from such language by understanding that we are allowing it to not only define us but also to limit us.

Your turn

Part 3: My self-limiting and self-supporting beliefs

My self-limiting beliefs	My self-supporting beliefs

Having seen your lists side by side, we invite you to reflect on what you have uncovered about yourself.

How are you feeling, and what are you noticing about yourself, having completed Exercise 1? Try to put this into words here, now.

Reflection

_____

_____

_____

_____

Now that you have named your problems – those which lie within your own self-limiting beliefs – and summarily dismissed or at least managed them, I invite you to have fun with the challenge of flipping the problems you really have to find a way to live with.

Declaring yourself capable of something **does not prevent** someone else being capable of it too!

Exercise 2: Flipping The Problem

Exercise 1 was aimed to help you see that your near-to-home problems, those of your own making, are often perceptions of yourself which need to be challenged and managed. Exercise 2 is concerned with those problems which arise in your world and may be out of your control. We pick up on Viktor Frankl's wisdom: that while you often cannot change these problems, you can change your attitude to them.

In the spirit of vulnerability ...

I have made choices in my life which, with the benefit of hindsight (20/20 I believe!), make complete sense to me. I even recognise that I *did* have a choice, however unapparent at the time that might have been. One of these choices was to remarry for love again as part of my search for unconditional love, freely given (which I have identified as one of my deepest yearnings). Despite this choice being evident to me now, along the way I bemoaned the fact that, although I married for love, I didn't have many of the trappings of material success. My problem sometimes may have looked like: 'If only I had a new car, a beautiful home with all mod cons, overseas holidays, blah, blah, blah ...'

Thank goodness I have now acquired wisdom through the work that Justin and I have passed on to you in this book, as I am able to own my decision and flip it into seeing my choice as the most releasing fulfilment of a fundamental need I have. I am rich indeed. My flip might be, 'How rich am I to have satisfied my deepest yearning?'

Part 1: Listing my 'If only ...'

Here are some examples of problems which others have experienced:
- If only I had more money ...
- If only it was up to me ...
- If only I had no fear ...
- If only no-one else needed to be involved ...
- If only I had more time ...
- If only I knew I couldn't fail ...

Your turn
Part 1: Listing my 'If only ...'

- If only _____

- If only _____

- If only _____

- If only _____

- If only _____

- If only _____

Part 2: Flipping my 'If only ...'

We have intentionally used a visual that represents 'below the line' and 'above the line' thinking. The 'line' represents thinking that serves your best interests. Below the line, therefore, is thinking that does *not* serve your best interests; and above the line is thinking that *does*.

Attitude that releases

the line ———————————————————————— **the line!**

Attitude that blocks

Examples:

In the two examples below, the attitudes that block were listed first, and then – through the skill of flipping – the attitudes that released were created.

Releaser: What can I do with the money that I have?

the line ———————————————————————— **the line!**

Blocker: If only I had more money ...

Releaser: Who else do I need to involve in this decision and how can I start the dialogue?

the line ———————————————————————— **the line!**

Blocker: If only it was up to me ...

Your turn

We invite you to flip four of your blockers.

the line ———————————————————— the line!

the line ———————————————————— the line!

the line ———————————————————— the line!

the line ———————————————————— the line!

AWE? (And what else?)

_____

_____

_____

_____

You are **reframing your constraints in a way that releases you** to begin to make change, to grow into your preferred self and realise your dreams, **one step at a time**. This is a way of reframing your attitude to serve you, not work against you.

Exercise 3: Vanishing The Problem

We hope you now recognise that some of your beliefs about yourself have been holding you back, but that you have the power to manage these beliefs and to change the attitudes that do not serve you.

Let's play with the idea that you can make your problems vanish and, in so doing, can imaginatively experience the changes of doing something differently!

Vanishing the problem is based upon the Miracle Question of Solution-Focused coaching, pioneered by Mark McKergow.

Scenario: You go to bed one night and when you wake in the morning, a miracle has happened: your problem has vanished. But, as you were asleep, you don't realise this straight away. What would be the first tiny indication that your problem is gone? Record your reflections below.

> # The aim is not to change what the client does, but to **change what the client sees as open to them.**
>
> *Mark McKergow*

Part 1: Signs of change

We invite you to imagine this miracle scenario happening to you. What has changed? What are you doing and saying? What are you noticing now that the problem has vanished?

Note: This is not an exercise in self-delusion, nor are we asking you to accept that we are in a new age of miracles. What we want you to notice is the effect on and changes in your behaviour when you take your gaze away from the problem – specific things you might *do*, or *say*, when the problem vanishes. The more you are able to imagine your changed behaviour, the more you will be able to imaginatively experience a release from your problems. This experience will raise your awareness of the behavioural changes you might want to bring into your life.

- _____

- _____

- _____

- _____

- _____

Part 2: Expanding the description

We now invite you to ask yourself these additional questions about what has changed when your miracle occurred. Be as detailed and specific as you can be.

- What difference would the changes make to person X?
- What would they do/say/feel when they noticed?
- How would you respond to person X?
- What happens next?
- Who else would notice the changes?

These expanders are helpful in reinforcing the fact that these changes in your behaviour, after the problem has vanished, will be noticeable to others! Play with this idea by imagining the significant people in your life noticing your changes. Be as detailed in your imagining as possible, as this will create an energising ripple for you as you imagine your life without the problems.

Speaking of energy; be aware of it when doing this exercise. PEA (Positive Energy Attraction) means that you are savouring and enjoying the problem-less state. NEA (Negative Energy Attraction) means that you have not managed to create this state, so make sure you have sufficient details that are concrete, specific, and behavioural.

Step 5: My Manifesto Draft Response

Having completed the exercises and reflected upon the information within *Step 5: The Releasing Step*, it is now time to write your draft response to the key question in this chapter.

What can I release myself from?

I can release myself from ...

Step 5: The Releasing Step – Case Studies

I can release myself from ...

The need to be perfect, and by doing so, model to others that a good enough, unique human being is perfect enough.

I can release myself from ...

My self-limiting beliefs: I can't protect myself; I have no choice; if I try I will fail; it's all pretend; smile though your heart is breaking; it helps to be quiet; I don't want to be in your way; you will make fun of me; I must care; nothing will help; enduring is enough; being useful is being used; don't let your feelings out or else; feelings are private; I can't feel this pain; sadness is overwhelming; you're smart, you must know; I can only wallow in my not-wallowing; I have to stay strong; others don't really care; trust them to be selfish; no-one will hold me; it's not safe; I'll be exposed; I'll hurt those I care about; I am unlovable.

My self-supporting beliefs can help my release: I can express myself, speak up, ask; I can choose; my centre is good and strong; I can trust myself to act because I'm okay and I care; I can survive, I can thrive; I am likeable; I am capable; I am considerate and gentle; I have friends and family who care about me; it is good if my needs are met (with respect); I can find what helps; I can relax and be vulnerable; I can enjoy; I can feel the pain and also the passion; I can encourage others; it's okay to be a bit selfish; I can let others see my flaws; I can be myself.

I can release myself from: hopelessness and helplessness.

I can release myself from ...

Self-limiting beliefs rooted in pessimism, worry, and fear of failure. I can release myself from doubt and stress and feel liberated by genuine confidence.

I can release myself from ...

My self-limiting beliefs, which include:
- I am not good enough.
- I am weak.
- I never finish anything.
- I don't have time.
- I should go last.

I can release myself from ...

Negative thoughts. Thoughts that can go on and on. I can bring in and access new ways to look at a challenge.

I can release the beliefs which hold me back, using my supporting beliefs to help work on it.

I can surrender the old beliefs to allow space for positive versions to enter.

I can release myself from ...

Limiting, disempowering, and sabotaging perspectives and beliefs by identifying them and consciously choosing to reframe my neurology. Shifting my mindset from a state of lacking to one of growth.

I can be mindful and intentional in the way I show up for myself via my thoughts, language and actions. Leading from a grounding place of self-empowerment, self-advocacy, and self-acceptance as I build upon my strengths, abilities, unique qualities, skills, and gifts.

I am committing to this daily through action and effort by being deliberate in my creation and supporting myself by using a variety of healing modalities that aid me in my perpetual holistic transformation.

7 The Contribution Step

6 The Connection Step

5 The Releasing Step

4 The Visionary Step

3 The Mattering Step

2 The Courageous Step

1 The Energising Step

Chapter 12:
Step 6: The Connection Step

Justin

Other people matter. Period. Anything that builds relationships between and among people is going to make you happy.

Wow! You are moving through these steps – nice work!

Back in 2000, I wrote my first ever personal mission statement. The second paragraph within this one-page statement reads:

'My relationship with Jeanette is the cornerstone of my happiness and I will strive to maintain and strengthen the interdependent marriage we have through ongoing listening and communication. With a strong marriage in place, I will feel confident in loving, caring, and teaching my family with all my heart. I want my children to experience unconditional love and I plan to work actively at bringing up happy, self-confident, and responsible children. I value deeply my extended family and close friends and I endeavour to fulfil my commitments in my various roles with enthusiasm and dedication.'

While written over twenty years ago, and when my wife and I only had one child, I speak of my 'plan to work actively' in my role as a father. There's that word again: 'work' – it's not referring to hard work, more just important work and work that will require enjoyable effort and attention.

The Harvard Study of Adult Development commenced in 1938 and is still running today. It is the world's longest in-depth longitudinal study on human life ever done. The findings from this research have led to a simple, yet profound conclusion from the current director, Robert Waldinger, that, 'Good relationships lead to health and happiness.' We are not surprised by this statement as we all intuitively understand how our relationships affect us physically and emotionally.

However, the trick is that our relationships must be nurtured. Just like it takes work and effort for us to maintain our fitness, it takes work and effort for us to maintain our relationships. So, given the importance of others in our lives, and the reality that tending our relationships takes considerable time, effort, and love, this chapter hones in on one powerful question.

The Connection Question

Who do I want to be known as?

Who: Not 'what' but 'who'. We are not asking about achievements, but rather about qualities.

I: As with previous questions, the central focus of this question remains you!

Want: We are interested in your preferences, your desires, and your choices.

Known as: Consider how you wish to be thought of, remembered by, and spoken about by others. This is your reputation; your character.

Exercise 1: My Social Web

We invite you to draw up your current social network, so that you can see and appreciate your treasured relationships.

Have you ever deeply considered the full range of roles that you have in your life? Below is a list of almost twenty roles – it is an extensive but not exhaustive list and we have also left several blank spaces for you to enter any other roles that are relevant to you.

Part 1: List of roles

Look over the list of roles below and highlight those that are relevant to you.

Partner	Neighbour	Sibling	Friend
Child	Team-mate	Parent	Cousin
Leader	Parent	Volunteer	Godparent
Pet parent	Daughter or Son-in-law	Mentor	Aunt or Uncle
Colleague	Sister or Brother-in-law	Grandparent	Grandchild
Coach			

With some roles, there may be various subsets of groups, for example: Friends – maybe friends you grew up with, friends from school, or friends from when you lived in a different town. You may well have colleagues from various workplaces. You may think of a past colleague more as a friend. Of course, all of this is fine; do whatever feels right to you at this current moment.

Part 2: Draw your social web

By referencing your roles rather than using specific individual names, draw a visual representation and connection of all your roles at this point in time.

We were going to start you off by placing 'ME' at the top of the following page, but then we thought that where you want to place this starting word may have a particular significance to you. So, you'll need to place a 'ME' somewhere on the page, and then enjoy drawing lines, arrows, circles, and any other relevant shapes or images that represent all the roles in your life at this moment. This 'social web' map will be completely unique to you. You may enjoy visualising particular people as you create your diagram. Enjoy.

My social web

Part 3: A deeper dive into two particular roles

We invite you to select two particular roles and reflect on what each role means to you, and how you wish to be in this role.

As you reflect, keep in mind that you cannot control the actions or behaviours of others; all you can control are your own actions and behaviours.

My role as a: _____

What does this role mean to me?	How do I wish to 'be' in this role?
What is one tangible act I could do to show the importance of this role in my life?	What do I receive from this role?

My role as a: _____

What does this role mean to me?	How do I wish to 'be' in this role?
What is one tangible act I could do to show the importance of this role in my life?	What do I receive from this role?

> **As an interdependent person, I have the opportunity to share myself deeply, meaningfully, with others, and I have access to the vast resources and potential of other human beings.**
>
> **Stephen Covey**

Striving For Interdependence Not Independence

We each begin life as babies, totally *dependent* on others. We are nurtured and sustained by others. We immediately start taking; we take food, we take air, we take comfort. Then gradually, over months and years, we become more and more *independent*, until eventually we can essentially take care of ourselves. For some people, they think this means they have made it – the ultimate goal of being independent. Can we suggest to you that there is a higher state? As we continue to mature and gain wisdom, we realise that life and nature are *interdependent*; that our relationships with others are vitally important and they, too, are interdependent.

Dependent people need others to get what they want. Independent people can get what they want through their own efforts. And, interdependent people can combine their efforts with the efforts of others to achieve great things.

I am extremely grateful for my interdependent relationship with Sue, from whom I receive so much wisdom and support. I am also grateful for my ancestors* who wrote down their wisdom that I could learn from; those who designed the computer so that I can type these words; those who enabled me to live in comfort with shelter, hot water, and electricity. I could go on, and I will: My parents, who filled me with love and inspired me to make a difference; my teachers, who taught me academic and life skills; and I am still only scratching the surface. To think that I have independently written this chapter would be far from the truth! 'We' have written this chapter, and I can't even fathom all the people who are an important part of that 'we'!

* The reference here to ancestors is literally fellow human beings who have come before us.

Exercise 2: Interdependent Me
....

This exercise invites you to reflect on key interdependent relationships in your life.

An interdependent relationship is where both people recognise and value a strong emotional connection, and also maintain a solid sense of self within the relationship dynamic. There is a healthy balance of independent selves and mutual reliance.

We provide room for you to reflect on three such relationships, but you can find printable templates on our website if you would like to consider additional people. We know you could write volumes about each person, but your challenge is to distil your thoughts down to one (or two) sentences for each of the four prompts.

My interdependent relationship with: _____

How has this person benefited me?	How have I benefited this person?
If this person was asked to describe me in one sentence, what would they say?	In five years' time, if this person was asked to describe me in one sentence, what would I like them to say?

My interdependent relationship with: _____

How has this person benefited me?	How have I benefited this person?
If this person was asked to describe me in one sentence, what would they say?	In five years' time, if this person was asked to describe me in one sentence, what would I like them to say?

My interdependent relationship with: _____

How has this person benefited me?	How have I benefited this person?
If this person was asked to describe me in one sentence, what would they say?	In five years' time, if this person was asked to describe me in one sentence, what would I like them to say?

AWE? (And what else?)

_____

_____

_____

P.S. You may also wish to write any of these people a gratitude letter, where you express how important and valuable their relationship is to you. Just a thought!

P.P.S. For interest, and self-awareness, you may choose to ask any of these people to actually describe you in one sentence. We wonder how similar their response would be to what you wrote.

Exercise 3: Character Strengths Mirror

Back on *Step 1: The Energising Step* we explored your Signature Strengths – your positive qualities which energise you, are relatively effortless for you to use, and feel essential to who you are.

Well, now that you are on *Step 6: The Connection Step,* we would like you to check in with a select number of people who know you well and seek their input on what are the highest positive qualities they see in you.

You may like to ask several family members, friends, and colleagues. Provide them with a list and definition of the twenty-four strengths and suggest they choose five key strengths they see in you. Of course, this may feel a little awkward, but it will provide you with rich insights. You may also like to return the favour.

In Appendix 4 you will find a sample letter that you can give to each of your strength spotters!

Strengths feedback

Reflection

- Having received feedback from your friends, what have you discovered?
- Did you uncover any strong Signature Strengths – strengths that were high on your VIA survey, and frequently recognised by others?
- Can you identify some 'strength blind spots' – strengths that were quite low on your VIA survey, but frequently recognised by others?
- And what about some 'strengths opportunities' – these are the strengths that are high on your VIA survey, but not regularly spotted by others. You have opportunities to action these particular strengths in a broader array of contexts.

Reflection

AWE?

Step 6: My Manifesto Draft Response

Having completed the exercises and reflected upon the information in *Step 6: The Connection Step,* it is now time to write your draft response to the key question in this chapter.

Write from your heart as you express your truth to the following question:

Who do I want to be known as?

I want to be known as ...

Step 6: The Connection Step – Case Studies

I want to be known as …

Someone who can be trusted to do the right thing at the right time for the right reason. I want to be known as someone who is fair and kind, somebody who is prepared to be honest, supportive and compassionate, even if that means tough decisions have to be made or complex discussions need to be had. I want to be known as someone who has wisdom and perspectives on life that can generate a sense of hope in all those I come into contact with as I journey through these last stages of life.

I want to be known as somebody who loved life, who was grateful for all I was given from my first breath until this very moment; sitting at this screen responding to this question. I want to be known as somebody who lived life with a passion, who adored nature and art and music and theatre and dance and the simple joys of life. I want to be known as somebody who tried to make a difference to the lives of others.

I want to be known as somebody who loved their wife and believed in the power of family – however one decides to define the concept of family in the twenty-first century. Whatever the definition, it must include love, kindness, safety, and a genuine a sense of belonging. I want to be known as a good citizen.

I want to be known as …

A loving, kind, and authentic person who sees, validates, and inspires others. I want to be known as someone with a deep desire to gain knowledge that enables my own growth and also enables me to inspire and empower others to grow.

I want to be known as …

- A loyal, caring, and happy friend.
- A confident, fun, and inspired person.
- A hard-working, intelligent, and brave worker and leader.
- A supportive and guiding sister.
- A grateful and caring daughter.

On my gravestone I want people to read …

She lit up the room with her warmth, hugs, humility, and love; she openly laughed and cried and lived a life full of adventures. She was a mother who hugged tight and long, who accepted, respected and loved us for our individuality, and was forever our cheerleader; she was a partner who was my best friend and the person who woke up each morning loving and supporting me unconditionally; she was a friend who listened without judgement and brought the fun to a night out.

I want to be known as …

A person who is loving and accepting – I want to create a safe space for vulnerability. For people, myself included, to feel heard, seen, and accepted. Create instead of chase.

I want to be known as a person who is dependable and authentic.

I want to be known as a person who is trustworthy and real.

I want to be known as a person who intentionally creates space for belonging.

I want to be known as a person who connects through authenticity.

I want to be known as …

A kind person and inspiring leader who is able to make others feel seen and heard and create safe environments where people can contribute meaningfully and feel comfortable to be themselves. I want to be known to inspire others to pursue their creative interests and to encourage others to realise their potential. I want to be known as a pragmatic dreamer, who dreams big and steadfastly works towards achieving their goals.

7 The Contribution Step
6 The Connection Step
5 The Releasing Step
4 The Visionary Step
3 The Mattering Step
2 The Courageous Step
1 The Energising Step

Chapter 13:
Step 7: The Contribution Step

Justin

The meaning of life is to **find your gift**. The purpose of life is to **give it away**.

Pablo Picasso

Bring on the *seventh step*! Having courageously explored each of the previous six steps, you are ready to consider the unique contribution you can make to others. We will explore individual others and groups of others, and we will ask you to draw upon the insights you have gained in your previous steps.

You have considered your Signature Character Strengths, your values, and what deeply matters to you. You have also envisioned your future, embraced your limitations, and reflected upon your connections. Now, it's time to meditate on how you can use your unique qualities to make a unique contribution to our world.

It is a privilege to make a positive difference in the lives of others. As Mahatma Gandhi was quoted to say, 'The best way to find yourself is to lose yourself in the service of others.'

Over the years, I have been very grateful to receive various thank-you cards from family members, friends, students, and colleagues. To warm my heart as I write this chapter, I reread an anniversary card from my wife, Jeanette. Despite being almost two years old, this card sits perched on my beside table. It goes like this:

> 'Happy 28th Anniversary. It is pretty incredible that we are old enough to be married for this amount of time. ☺ Thank you for your support, particularly this past year when teaching has become somewhat crazy. I feel very grateful that you are always there for me when the going gets tough. Thank you for being such a great Dad to our four beautiful children. It brings me so much joy to see how much they love you and appreciate all that you are. Thank you for planning our future together, thinking of ways that we know will be so much fun to do together. Looking forward to a lifetime of shared times and much love still to come.'

This step invites you to consider consciously engaging in activities for the benefit of others. You may consider your family, your friends, your work, your community, and your fellow humans. This step is about what you can give, as, in the wisdom of a young Anne Frank, 'No-one has ever become poor from giving.'

The question we wish for you to ponder as you progress through the exercises within this chapter is:

The Contribution Question

Who contribution do I hope to make?

What: Again, we invite you to generate a list of items; a list of possibilities.

Contribution: This refers to benefiting others, and it counts even if the others don't notice or know about your efforts. Consider both short-term and long-term contributions.

Hope: We seek your hopes. At this stage it's not necessarily a 'will I make …?' Rather, it is your plan – the contribution you are hoping to make.

Make: This requires personal action, effort, possibly sacrifice, most likely commitment, and only becomes a reality through tangible deeds.

An Attitude Of Gratitude

Gratitude involves appreciating the good things in life and recognising that they come from someone else. It is important to understand that there are two key aspects to gratitude: the first is experiencing (or feeling) gratitude, and the second is expressing (or acting on) gratitude. We like to think of gratitude as being a practice, because it is something we need to continue to work on throughout our days, our years, and our lives.

Gratitude can help us overcome our own feelings of fear and anxiety. As we adopt an attitude of gratitude towards ourselves, we can quieten our inner critic, improve our self-talk, and in turn become more compassionate towards others. This compassion can then assist others to ease their fears and be more grateful towards themselves.

A powerful activity is to complete a 'Gratitude Challenge from A to B'. A and B are simply any locations. For this example, let's consider A to be your home and B to be your workplace. Therefore, your challenge is to recognise and appreciate all the things that you have been given to be able to undertake this journey. The task, to notice *all* the things, is impossible, but you can certainly make a good fist of it.

While we don't know the details of your commute, we wonder if any of the following 'gifts' are relevant to enable you to get from A to B?
- The mechanic who tunes and maintains your car.
- The engineers who designed and built the roads and bridges you drive over.
- The traffic safety officers who monitor the road rules.
- The manufacturers who created your umbrella.

- The sheep who provided wool for your warm jacket.
- The musicians who produced the music you listen to.
- The satellite navigation system that provided you with the latest traffic report.

A.J Jacobs took this gratitude exercise several steps further! The premise of his latest book, *Thanks a Thousand*, was based on his challenge of travelling around the world to personally thank every person who made even the smallest contribution to his morning cup of coffee. This turned out to be over 1000 people and included coffee bean farmers, truck drivers, logo designers, and of course the barista!

Exercise 1: Ten 'Gifts' I Am Grateful To Have Received

Before thinking about the ways you can give to others, we invite you to pause for a moment and think about some of the many things you have received.

You may choose to focus on the immaterial gifts you have received, and/or continue to receive from family and friends. Alternatively, you may choose to focus on the material gifts for which you are grateful. You may like to consider your mentors, or people who have come before you, who you may or may not even know. This aligns with Sir Isaac Newtown's view that, 'If I have seen further, it is by standing on the shoulders of giants.'

Of course, as you consider your 'gifts', you may wish to combine ideas from each of the above approaches. We know ten is not nearly enough, but we hope you will enjoy compiling a sample of your unique and treasured 'gifts'.

Gifts I have received:

1. _____
2. _____
3. _____
4. _____
5. _____
6. _____
7. _____
8. _____
9. _____
10. _____

AWE? (And what else?)

_____

_____

_____

You started this journey with *Step 1: The Energising Step* to discover your unique Signature Strengths. We hope that each subsequent step has also provided you with additional energy, confidence, and inspiration.

And now, having just compiled your list of ten treasured gifts, we anticipate you are bursting with energy! What better way to harness this energy than to consider how you can take action that serves others and how you can give back.

Note: When compiling a list of 'gifts we have received', it is common to experience feelings of warmth and appreciation; however, feelings of indebtedness can also arise, which can also cause people to feel overwhelmed. If this is the case for you, you may prefer to consider how you can 'pay it forward' (or, as we like to say, 'live it forward') rather than 'paying it back'.

> **We make a living by what we get. We make a life by what we give.**
>
> **Winston Churchill**

Exercise 2: Going MAD – Making A Difference!

A helpful way to think about contribution is considering the difference you wish to make. We all have a tremendous opportunity, and a responsibility, to make a constructive difference to our loved ones, our neighbours, and our world.

We have no doubt that you are already making a meaningful contribution to others. As you consider this exercise, please list things that you are currently doing, or things that you have previously done.

While of course there are no limits to the contributions you can make, for the purpose of this exercise, we are constraining your list to *three* main contributions for each of the following three contexts.

Context 1: Your near and dear

As you bring to mind close loved ones and dear friends, consider: How do you, and how can you, make a difference in their lives? Vying for your three choices may be ways you can make people feel (safe, loved, confident, at ease …); ways you can offer support (companionship, sounding board, jobs …); or ways you can provide, enable, empower, or inspire.

Three ways I can contribute to those near and dear to me are:

- _____

- _____

- _____

Context 2: Your neighbours and colleagues

We now invite you to turn your mind to people you know and connect with in your community. These may include your neighbours, colleagues, and team-mates. Let's ask the question again: How do you, and how can you, make a difference in their lives? You may consider ways you can show up for these people, ways that you can assist their growth, ways that you can lead, and ways that you can follow.

Three ways I can contribute to my neighbours and colleagues are:

- _____

- _____

- _____

Context 3: Your fellow global citizens

Our third context is considering fellow humans: people who you may just come into occasional contact with (a customer, a barista, a service provider, a fellow public transport rider …); or someone you may never know (someone who receives a blood donation, someone who benefits from a charity organisation, someone who enjoys nature and the environment …).

How do you, and how can you, make a difference in these people's lives?

- _____

- _____

- _____

The reason for inviting you to reflect on how you do, and can, make a difference in the lives of others is to grow your awareness of being 'other-oriented'. A general outlook of, 'How may I be of benefit?' can forge strong bonds between individuals, cultures, and communities.

We acknowledge there is a paradox of service – that in giving to others we also give to ourselves. This strong two-way connection between helping others and helping ourselves is self-generating. The more we help others, the happier we become, and the happier we become, the more we want to help others. However, it is also important not to neglect our own happiness for the sake of living for others.

Unhappy people are less likely to be benevolent, which then leads to further unhappiness. On occasions, it is important to take a birds-eye view of your life and to consider your current balance or imbalance of caring for others and caring for self.

Acknowledging Personal Challenges

Before we explore our final exercise, we wish to acknowledge that some, possibly many, and maybe even all of us go through difficult experiences and challenging times. For some, even thinking about contributing to others may feel out of reach due to the personal difficulties they are facing in their own lives.

Inspiring author and psychologist Maria Sirois compassionately helps readers navigate life's difficulties in her book, *Happiness After Loss*. Her writing and personal stories honour the emotions of grief, sadness, and loss, while also charting a path forward to hope and love.

When Maria was asked in an interview, 'What is the meaning of life?', her response was:

> 'To become awake and aware enough to find a way to love our lives, no matter how hard, and from that place of living, return love through generous hearts, open minds, and caring spirits. Rumi once wrote, "We are all just walking each other home." No matter how difficult our lives, how harsh our histories or limited our choices this we can do: we can find a way to walk at least one other being home once we have found a way to come home within ourselves with love.'

Whenever I read this paragraph I feel a rush of hope. I know that we all matter, and I believe that we can all make a difference, even when these differences run alongside the personal challenges we face.

When you make a difference in the lives of others, you feel a sense of connection with something greater than yourself. This is an incredibly powerful feeling. Is there a way that some of the differences that you make can have more of a lasting impact; can they become a part of your legacy? It is this concept of a legacy mindset to which we now turn our attention.

Exercise 3: Being A Good Ancestor

We find ourselves in a world plagued by short-term thinking, which causes many negative impacts on our species and our planet. Here, we invite you to carry out some long-term thinking, a skill espoused by philosopher Roman Krznaric in his powerful book titled *The Good Ancestor: How to think long term in a short-term world*.

The premise of the book is that the most important question we can ask ourselves individually, and collectively, is 'How can we be good ancestors?' What this question demands us to consider is how we can live in such a way that future generations will speak of our wisdom.

In the previous exercise, your contribution was generally couched in terms of the present moment. Now, we wish to stretch your timespan and encourage you to consider your contribution to those still yet to be born. How can you become a giver of gifts to future generations?

Part 1: Working long-term contribution

We invite you to think about the contribution you can achieve through your work life. What lasting impact can you make? What can be a part of the legacy you create and leave behind through your work?

_____

_____

_____

_____

Part 2: Personal long-term contribution

We invite you to think about the contribution you can achieve through your personal life. What impact can you have on younger generations? What positive social changes can you be a part of? What example can you live?

_____

_____

_____

_____

Step 7: My Manifesto Draft Response

Having completed the exercises and reflected upon the information within *Step 7: The Contribution Step*, it is now time to write your draft response to the key question in this chapter.

What contribution do I hope to make?

I hope to contribute by ...

Step 7: The Contribution Step – Case Studies

I hope to contribute by ...

Offering my time to share my acquired knowledge and wisdom with younger generations as well as sharing my insights with older generations, and I would like to continue offering and exchanging knowledge throughout my life.

I would also like to contribute to the world by inspiring the people who come into my life to pursue a creative career or connect with a creative practice in their personal lives if they have any inclination to do so.

I would like to always be kind to others and to treat others with respect throughout my life.

I hope to be a good example, mentor, and source of inspiration for women from varied and diverse cultural backgrounds like me.

I hope to contribute to the greater good of the world by ...

Embracing my passion of sustainable and reusable fashion, starting my business in this sphere and thereby reducing waste. With small steps, I want to steer the world away from a culture of fast fashion.

I hope to contribute also to the lives of the people I love by being a supporter of their dreams, by being a good listener to their problems, and offering time and love when they need it most.

I hope to contribute by ...

Planting seeds of new growth for the past, present, and future.

I hope to contribute by reminding humanity that we are the answer and that we have everything we seek in others. Teaching them the lost wisdom of our ancestors and ancient times, to reconnect with self, and tap into ourselves as an energy source of healing, guidance, and love.

I hope to contribute by ...

Supporting and empowering others to be free to be their unencumbered selves.

I am grateful to have received: growing up in my family of origin; my first kiss; musical bliss; our children and their feedback; books and podcasts; good advice from many bosses; thoughtful therapists; my camera; wonderful friends; my healthy body and mind.

I hope to make a difference by helping friends know that someone has their back; helping parents; helping kids get established.

I hope to make a difference by gardening for my eighty-four-year-old neighbours, mentoring work colleagues to feel confident, and by passing on knowledge and experience.

I hope to make a difference by protecting the environment and helping people tell their stories.

My long-term work contribution is towards a more sustainable world.

My long-term personal contribution is increasing connections in an increasingly fractured society, allowing the better angels of our nature to fly.

I hope to contribute by …

Living an authentic life which models giving and receiving love and kindness. I am deeply drawn to empowering and supporting others by being of service in a way that lets them shine their light, gain insight, and gain inspiration.

I hope to contribute by …

Being a mindful consumer of limited natural resources e.g. water, coal, et cetera.

I also hope to contribute by caring for people and making their lives easier and more comfortable through advancing technology and education, and for colleagues to have a safe and respectful work environment-mentorship program, avoiding burnout, bullying, and hierarchy.

Chapter 14:
My Unique Manifesto

Sue and Justin

With your newfound clarity, it's time to draft and then finalise, **for this moment in your life**, a unique manifesto that inspires, excites, motivates, centres, and guides **you**.

Congratulations – you are now ready to create your personal manifesto! And what a journey it has been. Every exercise you have completed has been about *you*! These exercises are also there for you to return to at any point if you need to spend more time on them.

It is now time to guide you through the process of pulling your insights together from the previous seven steps as you create your personal manifesto and sensitively format words and sentences that speak to you. There are three key actions to complete within this chapter – combining, refining, and creating.

Action 1: Seeing Your Draft Responses

Your initial task is to transcribe your draft response from each of the seven steps onto the one double-page spread. There are two main purposes for inviting you to do this transcribing task. The first is to provide you with an opportunity to simply revisit each of your responses. As you reread and rewrite each response, spend time appreciating the phrases and words you have used. This is not the time to change any words, simply to revisit them. You may have completed previous steps several days or several weeks ago and we are sure you will find it valuable to review each of your responses again. The second purpose is to allow you to easily compare and contrast each of your responses; you may see similar themes coming through, you may notice important differences, you may find valuable connections between different steps.

At the completion of this action what you will have in front of you is what we refer to as your 'raw material'. This is the collective fruits of your work across the seven steps. Can you begin to see these responses connect, integrate, and support one another?

Please go ahead and rewrite each of your draft responses on the following two pages.

Action 1: Seeing Your Draft Responses – My Raw Material

Step 1: The Energising Step

My Signature Character Strengths include …

Step 2: The Courageous Step

I stand for …

Step 3: The Mattering Step

I care deeply about …

Step 4: The Visualising Step

I dream about …

Step 5: The Releasing Step

I can release myself from ...

Step 6: The Connection Step

I want to be known as ...

Step 7: The Contribution Step

I hope to contribute by ...

Reflection ...

On seeing my seven responses together, I recognise ...

Action 2: Refining Your Responses
....

Nice work on Action 1. Maybe it's been two hours, two days, two weeks, or two months since you worked your way through each of the seven steps, completed the exercises, and provided your 'draft' responses. Having just rewritten each of your responses on the previous two pages, you may now find that you would like to tweak or refine some of your responses. This is completely fine and understandable. It's possible a later step provided you with fresh insight to an earlier step, or maybe as you sat with your draft responses, new insights arose.

Your refined responses may be shorter or longer, you may change a word here or there, you may choose to emphasise a different angle, or you may choose to leave it exactly as it is. All of this is fine and an important part of your journey toward creating your manifesto. Before we invite you to refine each of your seven responses, we encourage you to take your time and consider how best to make your words *sing*.

Sitting With It

'Sitting with it' is the expression we use to remind us of the value of allowing an idea or indeed a response to percolate, brew, and simmer within your mind. Now that you have your manifesto responses all in one spot, sit with them and feel their energy for you. This is important. Remember, there is no rush. This time spent with your words allows you to decide – through all your layers of head, heart, and spirit – whether these responses truly reflect who you are and what you stand for and the life you're choosing to lead. Is there anything to add now that you have seen it all together? Is there any change you need to make? Take your time.

Making It Sing

'Making it sing' is the expression we use to remind us of the importance of smoothing and making a rhythm from your chosen words so that when you read them – and in our cases, and maybe yours – recite them as mantric phrases, they are pleasing to the ear and elevating to the spirit.

Run these dot points past yourself as you ponder your revisions:

- As you reread your draft responses, which words particularly sing for you? You may like to underline them.
- Are there words that stretch and challenge you? Consider choosing at least some of these, but not too many at the same time, to avoid NEA (Negative Energy Attraction).
- Are there words that comfort and support you? Self-compassion is important as you guide yourself.

- Has a metaphor that resonates arisen for you during this work? A mental image can evoke a pleasing visual which motivates you.
- Is there a way to repeat a common phrase or sentence starter? This can effectively generate a rhythm that sings to you.
- Combining two or more ideas, even if they may appear at first to be opposing ideas, with 'and', can convey the possibility of dual meanings – for example, 'Life contains beauty *and* chaos.'
- Use a thesaurus for synonyms to key words if you want to see words other than the ones you have thought of.
- Read your words aloud so you 'hear' them. Are they rhythmic? If they don't fit, choose an alternative word that suits the rhythm.
- Do you feel the truth of your words? That goosebump, that tingle?
- Does the punctuation you have chosen assist the meaning? This is a matter of scanning: when reading it aloud, do you stumble on some words? Are the sentences so long that you find yourself losing the meaning? Does the emphasis land on the wrong words so that your meaning is not clear?

Experiment with the punctuation:

- A comma assists your meaning with pauses as you intend.
- A colon introduces a list.
- A semicolon balances two related parts of a sentence, without a connecting word, so that they inform each other.
- A full stop adds power and significance.

I continue to be inspired by Sue's use of language and expansive vocabulary. Her many years of studying and teaching literature have resulted in what I find to be a rich and beautiful command of our language. I suggested to Sue that she could prepare a list of one hundred uplifting and inspiring words that can be relevant for this work – you will find her list in Appendix 6, and you will notice that she couldn't stop at one hundred!

Please take from this message of 'making it sing' the encouragement to use and harness words that resonate for you. It is not about the complexity or the sophistication of the language; it is about using phrases and terms which have a PEA (Positive Energy Attraction) for you.

Please go ahead and refine each of your draft responses on the following two pages.

Action 2: Refining Your Draft Responses – My Refined Material

Step 1: The Energising Step

My Signature Character Strengths include ...

Step 2: The Courageous Step

I stand for ...

Step 3: The Mattering Step

I care deeply about ...

Step 4: The Visualising Step

I dream about ...

Step 5: The Releasing Step

I can release myself from …

Step 6: The Connection Step

I want to be known as …

Step 7: The Contribution Step

I hope to contribute by …

Reflection

On seeing my refined seven responses together, I recognise …

You now have your refined material! We hope separately and collectively these are a powerful set of words, thoughts, beliefs, and hopes which inspire and guide you.

Five Personal Preferences

You are so close, but before you create your current personal manifesto, we would like you to answer each of the following prompts with your current preference. Please note there are no 'right' answers – it is simply personal preference for where you are at right now! You are most welcome to repeat this process at a different time, with different preferences, resulting in you constructing a different version of your personal manifesto.

Question 1: I would like my manifesto to be approximately as long as:
[ ] One page   [ ] One paragraph   [ ] One sentence

Question 2: I envisage the following people 'seeing' or 'reading' my manifesto:
[ ] Only me   [ ] Just a few people   [ ] Quite a lot of people

Question 3: The steps and responses which I particularly hope to emphasise are … (Please select as many as you wish):
[ ] Step 1   [ ] Step 2   [ ] Step 3
[ ] Step 4   [ ] Step 5   [ ] Step 6
[ ] Step 7

Question 4: At an overarching level, I view my manifesto as being mainly for:

[ ] Me   [ ] Me and my family   [ ] Me and my colleagues

Question 5: If I choose to display my manifesto, I envisage displaying it in the following ways:

[ ] On a wall   [ ] On a desk   [ ] On a screen   [ ] Other

Action 3: Creating Your Current, Personal, Unique Manifesto

Guess what? It's time! Like, literally now! If you feel you are in the correct headspace and in the right environment, we know you are ready. We know you have done 'the work'.

Taking your refined responses to each of the steps, and taking into account your personal preferences and your tips for making it sing – simply go ahead and choose the words, phrases, sentences, or paragraphs to write something that inspires you, that feels right to you, that will support you to live your authentic life.

You may take some words or phrases from each of your seven responses, or you might just focus on one response for your current manifesto. Whatever you decide, your current manifesto is the guide through which you will calibrate the crossroads of your life. Use it and know that this is you living as your most congruent and highest self.

There are absolutely no hard and fast rules to abide by when writing your final version. Please only take on the advice that helps – it could be all of it, or only one part! *You* construct *your* manifesto.

Note: Your personal manifesto represents you in this moment. As you change and life's circumstances change for you, different parts of your raw or refined material may 'call to you'. When the time feels right, you can design a new current version. Ensure you date it because you are charting your life's journey in each variation! All manifestos, as we stated in *Part 1*, are both stable and dynamic. Some of your words may still work for you and some may need replacing. Enjoy the renewal of that dynamism. You are evolving you.

It's time to create your current, personal, unique manifesto! Enjoy!

My unique manifesto

_____

_____

_____

_____

_____

_____

_____

_____

_____

_____

_____

_____

_____

_____

Dated:

3

LIVING
YOUR MANIFESTO

Chapter 15:
Living Your Manifesto

Justin

Your future is in good hands ... yours! Do you agree?

Hi!

You've made it! You've created your current, personal, unique manifesto. Go you! We hope you feel proud of and empowered by the document you have created and the insights you have gained throughout the process. But wait – there's more.

You may remember that we concluded *Part 1* with a chapter titled *Our Pep Talk*, and now we commence *Part 3: Living Your Manifesto* with a related chapter titled *Your Pep Talk*.

We are not sure if it has been days, weeks, or months since you read Chapter 6, *Our Pep Talk*, and we are also unsure as to how you are feeling about your recently completed personal manifesto.

In *Part 1* – the priming chapters – we had a chapter titled *Starting Where You Are At*. And now, as we embrace *Living Your Manifesto*, the same principle applies: let's start living your manifesto where you are at! For some of you, your manifesto will be a concise and clear expression of what deeply matters to you. It might align nicely with your current life and therefore not require much change from you. For others, you may have newfound clarity that requires new routines, different priorities, or changes of some sort. Either way, let's just start where you are at!

We enjoy the term 'pep', but we appreciate that the style, amount, or flavour of your pep is a personal preference – this is why this chapter is titled 'Your Pep Talk'. Some people like still water, others like it lightly bubbled, others love it as sparkling as possible. And some don't even like water!

Hopefully, you are now becoming quite familiar with the concept of coaching yourself, and while it is not easy, you can determine what is best for you and how you best like your 'pep talk'.

Some Starting Points

Still water pep talk

- I look forward to small signs appearing that show me ways I am living my manifesto.

Lightly bubbled pep talk

- I suspect there will be moments when I don't live according to my manifesto, and that's okay. However, I know that I can revisit my manifesto at any time, recognise the words and phrases I have personally crafted, and use them to intentionally lean into living tomorrow.

Sparking pep talk

- I choose to read my manifesto on a daily basis and to reference the wisdom that lies within it, particularly as I make important decisions or when I am faced with certain dilemmas. I look forward to sharing aspects of my manifesto with my loved ones and believe this will help them to both understand and support me.

No water pep talk

- Manifesto: tick! Let's crack on.

Some people adopt a view that motivation doesn't last, so it isn't worth the effort. For us, this is a little bit like someone saying, 'Staying clean doesn't last, so it isn't worth the effort of having a shower.'

It is true – motivation comes and goes, ebbs and flows, and we need to understand and appreciate this. Personally, we find that rereading part or all of your personal manifesto can be a great way to rekindle your motivation, which in this case is your commitment to living your authentic life; a life that is meaningful and fulfilling to you.

Do you remember our 'real guarantee' from *Our Pep Talk*? As we invite you to read it once again, do you feel confident that your manifesto can assist you in such ways?

Our Guarantee

We are confident that your manifesto will:

- minimise internal conflict;
- help you navigate life;
- build hope;
- raise your awareness of what is important to you;
- provide greater clarity in your life;
- uncover rich personal insights;
- assist you to make difficult decisions.

If you were to write one statement on how this process and/or your manifesto can support you, what would you write? You are welcome to choose any of the seven bullet points above or to create your own phrase.

Dream as if you'll live forever. Live as if you'll die today.

James Dean

Coaching Yourself In Difficult Times

If things are going well for you, coaching yourself will probably be relatively easy, so let's turn our attention to focusing on when things *aren't* going so well.

Of course, your manifesto will not protect you from things going wrong or from disappointments, setbacks, challenges, and adversities which appear in your life. And, just like your manifesto, you will continue to be unique and imperfect.

So, how can your manifesto help in difficult times and how can you best help yourself in such times?

When coaching yourself, you need to ask yourself the question, 'What is best for me at this moment?', and the answer won't always be to 'let it go', or 'go easy on yourself', or 'it doesn't really matter'. The answer also shouldn't always be to 'keep persevering', or 'be hard on yourself', or 'catastrophise'. The trick, or the skill, for any coach is to determine what is best for the coachee.

Another question that arises, when considering what is best for the coachee (in this case, you), is, 'Should I be thinking about what's best in the short-term, or best in the medium- to long-term?' We wish we had an answer for you! But simply being aware that your answer may differ will assist you in striking a healthy balance.

So, you have your responses to the twenty-one exercises, you have your raw and refined material to each of the seven questions, and you have your current manifesto. When you are experiencing difficult times, it may be helpful to revisit one of the particular exercises. You may reread some of your refined paragraphs to discover a jewel in there that feels particularly pertinent given what you are going through.

Let me just pause here by revisiting those words – 'what you are going through'. Would it be okay if I added two letters and changed this to 'what you are **grow**ing through'? It's common for all of us to have things we are 'going through'; this is often referred to as our 'common humanity', and some of these things can be extremely difficult and challenging for individuals, families, or communities. So, while they may be common, that certainly doesn't mean they are easy, and we don't want to minimise the challenges you may be going through.

But I wonder if, like me, it can help to add just two letters – instead of reflecting on what you are *going* through, you may reflect on what you are *growing* through. It may not make things any easier, but it still helps you consider how you can grow in response to the challenges you are facing. Maybe you can grow in wisdom, compassion, or resilience. And, of course, don't hesitate to let others help you as you go through (I mean 'grow' through) whatever you're facing.

Now back to what can help in difficult times: one is accepting our 'common humanity' as we have just highlighted; another is accepting 'your humanity'; and a third is accepting 'what is outside your control'.

Acceptance

Accepting our 'common humanity' means that we acknowledge that we are all humans, facing similar problems. We all experience suffering, stress, loss, and pain at stages in our lives. These are core components of what make us human.

The opposite of accepting your common humanity is the experience of isolation: the feeling that your emotional pain, your flaws and failures are inherent only to you. This poses a threat to your sense of belonging, whether it be your belonging in families, in communities, or in humanity.

Accepting 'your humanity' means that you practice forgiving yourself for your flaws. You accept that you aren't perfect and recognise that you have limitations and shortcomings.

Accepting 'what is outside your control' requires you to firstly consider what actually lies *within*, and what lies outside your control. We must appreciate that many things are simply outside of our control. We can choose to fight them, dwell on them, push against them, or we can choose to accept them.

What we *can* control is our own actions, our own behaviour; we can choose how we wish to express our manifesto, and we can choose how we wish to live.

We hope that we haven't made this concept of acceptance sound too easy. It is hard, and it takes courage and practice. One skill that can be of great assistance in this quest is self-compassion.

Self-Compassion

In a nutshell, self-compassion simply means extending our compassion for others to ensure we hold compassion towards ourselves. Kristin Neff, a leading researcher in this field, describes self-compassion as 'a self-attitude that involves treating oneself with warmth and understanding in difficult times and recognising that making mistakes is part of being human.' You will recognise the similarities here with embracing our common humanity, which is one of the three interrelated components of self-compassion. Each component has two parts: the presence of a helpful approach and the absence of an unhelpful approach.

The three components are:

- Self-kindness: Being kind and understanding toward oneself *rather* than being self-critical.
- Common humanity: Seeing one's fallibility as part of the larger human condition and experience *rather* than isolating.
- Mindfulness: Holding one's painful thoughts and feelings in mindful awareness *rather* than avoiding them or over-identifying with them.

Self-compassion is not 'self-indulgence' or 'self-pity'; it is treating yourself in a similar way as you would treat a close friend, or how a close friend would comfort you when facing adversity.

As we raised in *Questions As Doorways*, we once again caution you not to sabotage or criticise yourself as you seek to live in accordance with your manifesto. Go gently on yourself as you continue along your journey – making mistakes, facing setbacks, and gaining fresh insights.

We highly recommend either of Kristin Neff's books on self-compassion and also Stanford University's Center for Compassion and Altruism Research and Education website for anyone seeking to learn more about this valuable skill.

Personally, I have found the following statements, commonly found within self-compassion meditations, to be both helpful and hopeful.

- *May I be safe.*
- *May I be kind to myself.*
- *May I be accepting of myself.*
- *May I be loving towards myself.*

Replacing the 'I's with 'we's, and the 'myself' with 'ourselves', provides a lovely second round through the statements.

One final suggestion: When things aren't going so well, please remember that you have all twenty-four Character Strengths at your disposal and in particular your Signature Strengths which are essential, effortless, and energising for you to use. When finding things difficult, don't hesitate to ask yourself, 'Which of my Signature Strengths could help me now?'

Questions We Invite You To Ponder

- What does your pep talk look and feel like?
- How can your manifesto assist you in difficult times?
- What is your current relationship with self-compassion?

Having uncovered your best self, now and long into the future is your time to live your best self. **Again, we believe in you!**

Chapter 16:
Small Steps And Great Small Steps

Sue

I long to accomplish a great and noble task; but it is my chief duty to accomplish small tasks as if they were great and noble.

Helen Keller

Part 3 of this book really came into being in response to a question which one of our **my manifesto** clients asked after they had completed their personal manifesto experience with me in the coached Zoom session. 'Alright, I have my personal manifesto now and I love it, but how do I *live* it?' This question really got to the nub of it.

Your personal manifesto represents your best self – the life you wish to manifest.

The journey to creating your manifesto began by recognising your Character Strengths, then progressed to recognising your values, and onward through the seven steps to discover your highest order self. We know that achieving and sustaining our highest order life requires daily acts of *will*. We need to choose and step into that life with intention.

As you do this, you will be challenged, buffeted, and tested in your resolve to be that person living that life you laid out in your personal manifesto.

The good news is you have your guide. And you know your direction.

Your personal manifesto – the current version – is a visible sign to yourself that *this is me*, this is what I stand for, and this is the life I choose to live. Every time you have a choice, a decision to make, make it with your manifesto as a guide.

Ask yourself the question, 'Is this choice congruent with my manifesto?'

If it is, and you can see yourself making a choice that emphasises your authentic self and your highest life, then make that choice! A helpful way of knowing that choice is the right one is judging the way you feel after having made it.

Is it a feeling of ease? Is it an inner comfort? Right choice!

Is it ill-ease? Stomach churning? Wrong choice!

A Note Of Caution

Checking in with your feelings, tapping into your intuition, your inner knowing, takes practice. If you are accustomed to doing this – sitting quietly and listening to yourself, the authentic voice within you – then you will be able to validate your choices in this way. If, however, it is a new practice, one you have not intentionally established as you rush through your busy life, it may be hard to hear yourself. It may also be hard to separate your choice from the fear that surrounds it. Be gentle with yourself. You know you. Start where you are at and gently teach yourself how to tackle the situation in stride.

Once you have your choice, your decision, it becomes your first small step towards living your manifesto life.

To reiterate, your personal manifesto represents your best self – the life you wish to manifest. Today, now, even though you were able to see that self and life and write it down eloquently in your personal manifesto, like the **my manifesto** mate who posed the opening question of this chapter, it is another thing entirely to live it! Where you are at is where you start, and each small step represents your progress on the journey towards actualising your manifesto.

A small step, one action, one decision, is how you make progress. It is very easy to overwhelm ourselves by thinking that today, with my personal manifesto, I have to revolutionise my life! I can feel the fear from here! *No!* The 'revolution', should it be needed (it may only be a ripple), will happen one small step at a time.

The wonderful Mark McKergow of *The Solution Focus Approach* has a mind-stretching addition to this idea for those who want to hasten their progress: make sure that small step is a great small step!

Five pointers for taking a great small step:

1. It is for me to do. It's not about getting someone else to do something.
2. It does not need someone else's permission to do it.
3. It is small enough to do in the next twenty-four hours.
4. It is generative, i.e. It should start something, not stop something; it should be something that is either engaging other people or at least visible to other people in some way.
5. I would notice over the next few days tiny signs of progress if the step is having a good effect.

Note: These five pointers help you to maximise your progress by ensuring your small step has maximum impact! It is also okay though if your pace is glacial, at least at first, as you build momentum! Meanwhile, any change, any movement forward, is progress. Where you are starting from and the size of the gap you wish to bridge may shape the rate of your progress. And many pages ago, we reminded you that this is not a competition. This is not the Manifesto Olympics! You are going for your own PB in your own race!

> If you are wanting to hasten your progress — make sure that small step is **a great small step!**
>
> *Mark McKergow*

Gentle Change

For many, if not most of us, change is scary. Our brains are programmed to resist change. When our brain detects a new challenge or opportunity or desire, it can trigger a degree of fear. Our brain, which is responsible for controlling our flight-or-fight response, would generally far prefer us to stick to our usual, safe routines.

When people want to change, they often go about it in a drastic way, hoping to achieve something we could refer to as 'radical change'. There is nothing wrong with this per se. When it works, this approach can produce amazing results. Each of us has likely experienced such positive change and growth by adopting more drastic measures. But the 'when it works' paradigm comes with risks, and this approach can also backfire.

A problem with radical change is that, despite often being met by early short-term success, we can so easily fall back to old ways and old habits once our initial burst of motivation and enthusiasm fades away. Often, people don't realise that there is another way to change – a way that is so gentle, you hardly even notice the change happening!

Welcome to an approach to change known as 'Kaizen', similar to McKergow's 'great small steps'. Kaizen is a Japanese term that comes from two Japanese words: 'kai', meaning 'change'; and 'zen', meaning 'good'. Therefore, it literally means 'good change', but it has also become synonymous with the concept of continuous growth and improvement.

The Kaizen approach to change is about taking small, safe steps to accomplish large goals. The process is designed for significant, lasting change. The well-known phrase, attributed to the ancient Chinese philosopher Lao Tzu, beautifully sums up the Kaizen approach: 'The journey of a thousand miles begins with a single step.'

Kaizen allows us to meet life's constant demands for change by seeking out continual, but always small, improvement. Kaizen strategies can include: asking yourself small questions; thinking small thoughts; taking small actions; solving small problems; bestowing small rewards; and recognising small moments.

The Follow-Through

When you have decided upon your first step, regardless of the size, it is important to take it! If you've had issues with follow-through in the past, what can you do to make sure you do follow-through now?

Take a moment to consider what strategies you already have in place to help yourself here.

- Do you keep a diary, electronic or paper? Are you a post-it note person?
- Do you tell a friend your intention? What do you do?
- Do you need to give yourself a deadline? *I will do this* … (signed, dated, or diarised!).
- How do you sustain your small step and make sure you do not drop your resolve when you hit one of life's speed bumps?

Remember, you are coaching you here. Of course, we are also here to coach you if you need us. We started out there, and took this wonderful journey of the book, but we have also never lost sight of our guiding leadership philosophy of servant leadership. What do you need now?

It is also important to note that a golden rule of coaching is that the agency, the responsibility for action and change, must remain with the person being coached: *you*! Please see this as a positive. No-one knows you better than you, and no-one knows what is best for you to do right now better than you.

This book aimed to help you become aware of who you are and the best life you can lead. You wrote your personal manifesto as a result. Now you must live it – the responsibility for that life is yours. We are responsible for our own lives; part of the way we choose to live those lives is in service to others, namely you.

So, recognise what you need to do to stay on your path; with this guide in hand, decide your first step, declare your intentions to take that step with an internal resolve or external accountability, and be on your way!

Questions We Invite You To Ponder

- What is the first step you will commit to?
- What is the next step you will commit to?

No-one knows you **better than you** and no-one knows what is best for you to do right now **better than you**.

Chapter 17: Shaping Your Environment

Justin

First we make our habits, then our habits make us.

John Dryden

Hopefully you can see that we are invested in assisting you to honour your personal manifesto. You've given yourself a pep talk that suits you, and we've shared the gentleness of preparing and performing your first step, as well as other related small steps.

We now turn our attention to the power of your environment and consider how we can help make change as non-threatening, as easy, and as effective as possible. It is likely that you have uncovered some insights which have led to you wanting to change some aspects of your approach, your attitude, and your priorities. Let's make sure your environment can help you with this.

Work On Your Environment

While of course it is important for each of us to care for the environment, and some of you may well have references to nature, mother earth, or sustainable development in your manifesto, here we are referring to *your* environment. This includes your home, your workplace, your neighbourhood, and even your culture, your family, and your friends.

We are easily, and often subtly and subconsciously, shaped by our environment, our setting. In this chapter we invite you to take a step back and consider various aspects that are present or absent in your environment.

Because our environment has a significant impact on us, then it makes sense for us to try to shape aspects of it so that we feel it is working in our favour – that it is helping us to live aligned with our manifesto.

James Clear, author of *Atomic Habits*, suggests that we do not rise to the level of our goals; rather we fall to the level of our systems. In the spirit of Clear's quote, it could go like this: 'We do not rise to the level of our manifesto; rather we fall to the level of our environment.'

So, you have your inspiring manifesto – what can you put in place to allow your environment to support you?

Let me give a quick example regarding my current focus of trying to drink two litres of water a day. I like drinking water, but I often forget. I have set myself the challenge of drinking two litres of water a day on many different occasions over the past decade and each time I've lasted a couple of days before I fell back into bad habits. I am motivated and focused in the beginning and due to my intention it is relatively easy for me to drink the goal amount of water, but then my focus wanders, my motivation drops, and my intention is lost.

However, my most recent effort appears to be having far greater success. A friend simply said to me – go out and buy yourself four x 500ml water bottles. Then, first thing each morning, fill your four water bottles and place them in strategic places you'll be throughout your day. You could place one in the kitchen, and one in the bathroom, one in the car, and one at work. Someone else might put one in the loungeroom or one in their shed, but I'm sure you get the point. Suddenly, through quite minimal effort, you live in an environment that makes it very easy for you to remember and to actually drink water! Your goal is simply to drink each of the four water bottles before you go to bed. It is not that you suddenly have a whole lot more motivation or willpower; you have simply 'shaped your environment' to make it easier for you to achieve something that was important and worthwhile.

I hope you can draw the parallels between my relatively minor example of drinking water with your relatively major example of your manifesto. We need our environment to help us.

Of course, it may not always be as easy as strategically placing four water bottles and it may well require some creativity on your behalf, but we strongly encourage you to give it a go!

Below we've listed ten possible changes to our environments that could assist with living authentically.

- Place photographs of loved ones around your home and/or work.
- Write reminders or messages on strategically placed sticky-notes.
- Change your computer password to a word that has particular significance (maybe it's a Character Strength or a core value).
- Keep technology out of your bedroom.
- Turn your TV around to face the wall every time you turn it off so that it takes extra effort for you to watch TV.
- Agree to meet a friend for your morning walk, run, or gym session.
- Set up a meditation chair that looks inviting and is easy to access.
- Limit your screen use through setting app limits or alarms.
- Find easy ways to bring more music into your home or office.
- Place your runners in the fridge! (Or just in front of the fridge door.)

The list is endless, but hopefully something has sparked for you.

Another way of viewing this concept is considering, 'What can I do today that will make it easier for me to live authentically tomorrow?' Is there something that you've been putting off, something that you could fix, or something you could put in place? For me and Sue, the simple change of setting up a Habit Share app on our phones with the joint goal of working on our book for at least thirty minutes a day held us accountable to one another and helped ingrain a consistent writing routine. This app certainly helped our change into becoming daily writers!

Helping Change Along

While you know first-hand that change can be hard, we also suggest that you know first-hand that people can and do change, and we suspect you can list multiple ways that you have changed in the past months, years, or decades.

Sue couldn't help but jump in here!

In the '80s I was teaching at a school in the Goulburn Valley, which was led by an enlightened principal, who would inspire us with his educational insights. On one occasion in his principal's address, he focused on the concept of 'change'. He was very energised, and I suspect he was responding to some negativity that had reached him about the difficulty of teaching certain students and a defeatism about their capacity to change their behaviour for the better. His words were:

'If we don't believe in the capacity to change, we don't deserve to call ourselves educators.'

Strong words I have not forgotten.

The moment you have experienced personal change or have seen someone else change, you will know that change is possible! Yes, it is often hard, which is why we would like to give you some strategies for helping your change along.

Changing With E.A.S.E

E – EASY
Consider how you can make your desired change feel as easy as possible. This may well involve shaping your environment in some way.
Ask: How can I make it easy for me?

A – ATTRACTIVE
Consider how you can make your desired change appealing to you; something you are looking forward to doing; something that is exciting.
Ask: How can I make it attractive to me?

S – SMALL
Consider how you can make a successful first step – we hope that *Small Steps and Great Small Steps* gave you some helpful hints here.
Ask: How can I make great small steps?

E – ENERGISING
Consider how you can be energised by your desired change; how can you apply any of your Signature Strengths or the wisdom you gained from *Step 1: The Energising Step*.
Ask: How can I make it energising for me?

Interestingly, if you are endeavouring to stop a particular behaviour, rather than introduce a particular action, then you can try and reverse the EASE acronym. You want to make the behaviour you wish to stop as **hard** to do as possible, as **unattractive** as possible, as **big** and challenging as possible, and as **exhausting** as possible. (We're sorry the opposite acronym – HUBE – isn't as memorable!)

A key message we hoped to get across in this chapter is that often the reason we do not live aligned with our manifesto is not because it is flawed, and not because you are flawed or lacking in willpower and motivation, but because your environment may be working against you rather than working for you. We hope you can enjoy experiencing some desired change in your life.

Questions We Invite You To Ponder

- What could you add to your environment to make living your manifesto easier?
- What could you delete from your environment to make living your manifesto easier?
- What can I do today that will make tomorrow easier?

Change is painful, but **nothing is as painful as** staying stuck somewhere you don't belong.

Mandy Hale

Chapter 18:
Listening To Your Environment
Sue

Synchronicity occurs at the intersection of your awareness, response, perspective, and action.

Andrea Goeglein

Back in February 2022 while we were still developing our ***my manifesto*** business and before the launch, we were writing blogs about all the wellbeing matters that arose for us, the books we were reading, and the trials with the clients who were road testing our exercises. On this day, I wrote a blog on synchronicity. It was actually a book recommendation for Chris Mackey's book, *The Positive Psychology of Synchronicity*. Mackey, a clinical and counselling psychologist, opened my eyes to the phenomenon of synchronicity, which I soon learned is not a new concept but stretches back to Carl Jung and beyond.

Mackey writes of synchronicity as '… the phenomenon of experiencing a striking and meaningful coincidence that connects our inner and outer worlds.' His book is '… designed to help you uncover the symbolic meanings behind uncanny coincidences, and especially the ones you experience personally.'

Synchronicity And My Manifesto

This phenomenon and practice became meaningful for us. We had been developing the concept of co-creating a personal manifesto for those who wanted to experience the joy of putting into words life statements that encapsulate who we are, what we stand for, and the lives we wish to lead. Put this work together with the revelation of synchronicity and we began to look for those meaningful coincidences and to unravel their symbolic meaning.

I digress ...

Before I show *how* the practice of synchronicity evolved to reinforce our chosen work, I want to digress briefly to another revelatory concept – for me – that arose as a result of this practice. It was the understanding that, if we could be enjoined to make meaning out of the uncanny coincidences that occurred in our lives, could we therefore make meaning out of ... well, *all* of our experiences?

Perhaps, to you, this notion seems blindingly obvious. But stay with me a moment as I remind you of my context. I inherited religious values and doctrine, an education in religious schools, a 1950s father, and a patriarchal society. My compliance was expected and rigorously enforced. While I spent much of my adult life examining these 'gifts' and searching for my own meaning, I never consciously gave myself permission to *construct* my own meaning. Until recently.

It is this permission that I gave myself, that we have offered to you as you construct your meaning when working your way through our 7-Step guide. Your personal manifesto does not have to replace entirely whatever meaning and practices you have already chosen and cherish. Rather, it is a way of integrating those existing meanings and practices so that they continue to serve you, strengthened by the new awareness this work evokes in you.

What you have now is **your version** containing the legacies you have been granted that you wish to **take forward with you.**

To return to synchronicity!

Fully aware now of the legitimacy of creating my own meaning, I reinforced my constructs by noticing signs from the world around me, both natural and human-made, and reflecting on what meaning I could make of them.

Another blog entry I wrote at the start of our **my manifesto** journey is entitled 'The White Magnolia Tree'. In this blog I playfully linked the beginning of our fledgling business with the first blooms of 2022 on my one-year-old white magnolia tree. I say playfully, because I am fully aware that this comparison is not one of 'uncanny' proportions to be eligible for Mackey's definition of synchronicity. However, it was lovely fun to make the comparison. I particularly wanted to borrow the associations of the white blooms, and apply them to our **my manifesto** business. As one of the oldest blooming plants on earth, the magnolia connotes endurance, reliability, and resilience – all qualities I wished upon our endeavour. Add to these qualities the associations of the white flower – purity, spirituality, and peace – and I had the most perfectly inspirational and aspirational symbol possible in this imperfect world!

A Few Snapshots

During the course of developing our business, I became attuned to noticing and interpreting signs from the world around me. I would like to share a few snapshots of these with you now to illustrate further what a comforting and enjoyable practice this has become.

Every day I go for two walks; one in the morning before breakfast and one in the late afternoon before dinner. As I return from my greater-block circuit and not far from my home gate, I pass a small reserve with some children's swings and open-grassed area for children and animals to run. Usually when I reach this point, I am deep in reflection. I have been mulling over plans for the day's events and for the next stages of this writing. I use Google Docs on my phone to capture my thoughts as I go.

So many times, as I walk past this reserve on my left, the rising sun has slanted through the trees and bathed me in light across my left shoulder, my face and body. I see and experience this as a blessing for what my day will bring. There is nothing 'uncanny' about this occurrence. It is approximately the same time of day, each day, and as there is a break in the houses, it is possible for the sun to shine through uninterruptedly. Still, what feels like a sudden shaft of sunlight as I leave behind the last fence and step further upon the path beside the reserve never feels like a surprise – but rather, a 'go well with your day' blessing.

On January 26, 2023, the Chair of the Australia Day Council, Danielle Roach, stated that each recipient of the honours demonstrated a spirit that, '… share[d] a common bond: using their life experience as a power for good, helping others around them and making the world a better place.' While I am not suggesting for one moment that Justin and I are candidates for Australia Day honours, I feel that we share that bond, too. Our shared philosophy of servant leadership is the driving force behind writing this book, and our practice distils what we have learned from co-creating, trialling, and living our own personal manifestos. We have used our life experiences as a power for good. We want to help others around us *and* we aspire to make the world a better place.

Upon reading Charlotte Wood's *The Luminous Solution*, I noticed her words, 'The electric delight of recognising difficult truths ... At a point of revelation like these, laughter can be an extraordinary tool of connection. It allows us to see that we are all human; we are all children; we all fail.' Yes indeed. There it is again. None of us is perfect. None of us is always integrated and adult; all of us need to lighten up! My inner child, of whom I have spoken of in these chapters, is heard; is seen; is soothed.

I now invite **Justin** to share a moment of synchronicity ...

Thanks, Sue. My main challenge is determining which example to use! I do feel I am more attuned to my environment and I find myself noticing moments of connection, and circumstances of synchronicity, far more frequently. I like Chris Mackey's description of synchronicity, which goes along the lines of '... noticing when you get a free kick from the universe.'

I've chosen, Sue!

I share my connections with Chris and Sue Mackey and their family as a range of beautiful moments of synchronicity over the past ten years.

Back in 2012, I was the Head of the Positive Education department at Geelong Grammar School (GGS) in Victoria, Australia. I was charged with implementing and sustaining a whole-school approach to the relatively new field of positive psychology. It was an exciting and meaningful time for me. Despite my passion for wellbeing, as a career mathematics and physical education teacher I felt somewhat out of my depth! Only several years earlier, GGS had the privilege of hosting

Professor Martin Seligman, the founder of positive psychology, live on campus for a period of six months and introduce the science of human flourishing to the entire school community. Exciting times, but I was certainly on the lookout for support.

This support came in the way of Chris and Sue Mackey. The Mackeys had decided to enrol their youngest, Ellie, into GGS and it just so happened that Ellie and our eldest, Sam, were in the same year level. I didn't know Chris or Sue, but a chance meeting at the Welcome to Middle School BBQ for parents on the school oval early in 2013 was the first of what would turn out to be many, many conversations. Chris is one of Geelong's leading clinical psychologists and has remained at the forefront of positive psychology for many years. I had found the support I was looking for.

More than ten years later, Ellie and Sam remain great friends. They ended up in the same day house at GGS where they shared a study, they both went to the same college at university, and they both continue to be in the same incredible friendship group that enjoys travelling together and supporting one another through the ups and downs of life.

Sue Mackey and I were fortunate to be participants together in a powerful year-long Certificate in Positive Psychology course (CiPP) led by the Wholebeing Institute. Here we shared many moments and Sue wrote her beautiful book titled *Positive Oncology* as a capstone project for the course. In the book, Sue shares her journey of being diagnosed with cancer and details a wide range of positive psychology strategies to foster coping skills and resilience. Our son Sam was diagnosed with an osteosarcoma (bone cancer) in 2011, and again our families were connected in their journeys.

While there are many more synchronous moments, I'd like to share just one more regarding Sue and Chris's son, Rowan. Fast forward to 2017, I was now the Director of GGS's Institute of Positive Education, and our team thought it would be great to do a positive education podcast series. The only problem was that we didn't know anything about recording podcasts. But, who had just purchased all the recording equipment and was looking to get into producing podcasts? It ended up that Rowan Mackey recorded and produced our entire podcast series! (We would also like to mention the *Psych Spiels and Silver Linings* podcast, which is the dynamic father-son duo of Chris and Rowan Mackey. Relatively recently they celebrated their hundredth show.)

Observing and harnessing moments of synchronicity can be a powerful way to listen to, and learn from, your environment. We encourage you to give it a go.

Questions We Invite You To Ponder

- What 'free kick' from the universe have you noticed recently?
- What can you learn from your environment that assists you on your journey?

Chapter 19:
Am I There Yet?

Sue and Justin

It is good to have an end to journey toward; but it is the journey that matters, in the end.

Ursula K. Le Guin

Am I There Yet?

It's easy to smile at this archetypal question, reminiscent of weary children in the back seat of the car – I remember the long drives as a child in the old two-toned green Plymouth, with only unrelieved desert of red earth and scrabbly salt bushes to look at. But it is a fair question to ask after experiencing a journey of any length.

Your journey has been considerable; we have asked a lot of you. You have had to dig deep into the innermost parts of your psyche. This has not always been comfortable. It was probably both demanding and tiring. It may have taken you hours or even days to complete. This question, then – 'Am I there yet?' – is definitely fair enough.

Justin and I have not asked you to do anything we have not done ourselves. We are aware, though, that we share a love of introspection and an excitement about uncovering what we *really* think and feel about, well, everything! You may have asked the leading question – 'Am I there yet?' – many times along the way in increasingly plaintive tones, like the weary child. We hope too that you had those other moments of awe, stillness, awareness, realisation, wonder.

You would by now also have realised that while we are living, our journey is never complete; that is the nature of living. However, you have a guide now. You have clarity and you are aware of your authentic life.

Where Is 'There'?

I have a magnet on my fridge inscribed with the word 'peace' that was given to me by a colleague. For more than twenty years this magnet has held up family photos, invitations, bills, notices, reminders, fines, our kid's artwork, and more! And, all the time that it was doing its job, it proudly shared a powerful message to me and my family.

Akin to the emotions of serenity and contentment, peace is often a sought-after experience, both physically and mentally. So much so that it is an integral message on many grave headstones, found within the letters R.I.P.

While on a very different scale, there have been times when I've yearned to make it to the end of my to-do list, longed to leave work with a clean desk, and wished that I was on top of everything at home with a pristine interior, healthy, happy and well-behaved kids, and of course an immaculate garden! But it is actually the message on my fridge magnet that helps me understand that this is not the goal, nor the destination, nor where I am seeking to arrive.

For me, this fridge magnet has regularly reminded me that peace is being in the middle of a meaningful and purposeful life, which is full of responsibilities, challenges, and opportunities. Peace is a place where there is noise, there is trouble, and hard work is required, but at the same time, you can feel and be calm in your heart.

When I hear people talk about 'being happy', I don't think they're really referring to in-the-moment happiness. Everyone knows that this emotion comes and goes, as it must, for us to appreciate it when it is present! I think in general, people are talking more about a deeper, long-term, or state of happiness, which I feel is much like the expression of peace.

For me, while Sue correctly points out that it is fair for a child to ask, 'Are we there yet?' on a long road trip, and fair that you may have had moments where you asked the same question during this book, I hope that you are also at peace with *not* asking this question about your life.

There is nowhere for us to arrive at, but there is a way to be. Through living in alignment with your manifesto, and harnessing the skill of mindfulness – including breathing practices which enable you to insert several pauses within your day – we can find that 'nowhere' can become 'now: here'. We can learn to be present within the midst of the noise of our lives and still experience peace.

Peace. It does not mean to be in a place where there is no noise, trouble or hard work. It means to be in the midst of those things and still be calm in your heart.

(Unknown) *Justin's long-standing fridge magnet*

What A Difference A Word Can Make!

I was recently reminded by a friend that simply changing one word in my vocabulary could assist me to cherish my life and to experience a greater sense of peace.

On hearing me say 'I have to mow the lawns', this friend reminded me that I could choose to say, 'I get to mow the lawns', rather than 'I have to'. Of course, one word is such a small difference, but gosh it can make a profound difference! On this occasion, it certainly helped to shift my mindset from one of obligation to one of opportunity.

Of course, there are many things we have to do in life, but when you choose to view them through the lens of opportunities, then you notice and remember the good fortune in your life. You can have new appreciation for your home, your family, your friends, your job – things we may often take for granted. Changing 'have to' to 'get to' can help jobs feel less mundane, moments feel more special, and can assist you to feel more present.

Do you know I **get to** …
- read another book;
- visit my mum and dad;
- take our dog, Maisy, for a walk;
- live my authentic life?

And, I will also get to revisit and redesign my personal manifesto from time to time over what I hope will be many years into the future. How lucky are we to have people to care for, things on our to-do lists, and a manifesto that we have personally created to guide and inspire us?

It reminds me of a well-known quote, often attributed to Tom Bodett, that says, 'A person needs just three things to be truly happy in this world: someone to love, something to do, and something to hope for.'

I'm still on the lookout for a fridge magnet with this quote on it, and then it can join my peace magnet and proudly hold up my current personal manifesto.

There is nowhere for us to arrive at, but **there is a way to be.**

With Our Warmest Wishes

I wonder if you feel like I do in that the lines from T.S Eliot's 'Little Gidding, Four Quartets' ring true:

> *We shall not cease from*
> *exploration, and the end of all our*
> *exploring will be to arrive where*
> *we started and know the place*
> *for the first time.*

We have said to you that you have your knowing, your knowledge, your wisdom, within. Our 7-Step guide draws forth what you know. As you lay down your responses and select your current iteration of your manifesto, do you feel the shock of recognition, the *Ah, this is me* awareness?

Don't feel discouraged when you realise that although you have climbed a mountain, as you look up, you are at the base of another. This is the adventure. Now, though, you are equipped because of the work you have done. We invite you to remind yourself of who you want to be, what you will stand up for, the attitude you choose to take, and the way you want to live. Be reassured you know your true self and that you have your eyes firmly fixed on your chosen road ahead.

To be honest, we're not sure how to finish this book, and to be perfectly honest, we're not sure if we want to finish this book. It has been both a joy and a challenge for us. We have loved every (well, most every!) session that we have sat down and put pen to paper, or finger to keyboard. We have enjoyed countless conversations and discussions together; we have gained gifts from our research and the wisdom of others; and now it is time to place a full stop at the end of this book.

But before we do, can we wholeheartedly wish you well! We hope through the work you have done that you feel: energised, courageous, and connected; along with a sense of lightness that comes from releasing oneself; and that you are clear in your vision of what matters to you as you live your authentic life: your contribution!

May you live with peace.

Sue & Justin

Further information and inspiration can be found at: **mymanifesto.me**

- Contact Sue and Justin
- Join the **my manifesto** community
- Print book exercise templates
- Purchase copies of the book
- View client manifestos
- Read the weekly **my manifesto** blog
- Enquire about speaking engagements
- Engage in **my manifesto** focus coaching
- Join a **my manifesto** retreat
- Learn about **our manifesto** for businesses

Acknowledgements

So many people have helped and supported us to create this book, and to make this process an accessible reality! Our heartfelt thanks goes out to every person who has enriched our journey, and to every expert who has generously shared their research and wisdom with us.

Thank you to our partners and soulmates, Gary and Jeanette, who have provided us with strength, reassurance, and love as we embarked on this journey. Our thanks also go out to our respective children, siblings and parents – it has truly been an extended family effort. We are so grateful to have benefited from the ongoing support, interest, and love from Joel, Dan, Jacquë, Sally, Chris, Margaret and Paul; and from Sam, Meg, Holly, Jack, Tony, Nicole, Tamara, Val and Gerry.

Thank you to our business partners, David Bott and Darren Loidl, at The Wellbeing Distillery for their financial assistance, business acumen, and unwavering support. It continues to be an amazing journey and we have the utmost respect and admiration for your skills and commitment. Put simply, this book would not be here without the two of you.

When we decided to pivot from our online experiences and write a book, we enlisted the support of Andrew Jobling, *Accidental Author*, as our book-writing mentor. His encouragement and passion and unwavering belief in us was and is a constant flame burning.

You can imagine our joy in receiving a positive email from experienced publisher, David Tenenbaum, on Thursday September 7, 2023. David founded Melbourne Books, a highly successful independent Australian publishing house that has been supporting authors and publishing unique stories for the past twenty-five years. Our excitement was further boosted after an initial online meeting with David when he shared his view that our manuscript was 'an unpolished gem'! Over the next six months, the team at Melbourne Books have carefully and professionally assisted us in the skill of polishing. In particular, our thanks go to Sophie Goodin, our dedicated and insightful editor, who got us and our book right from the start. We are extremely grateful for our close working relationship with the team at Melbourne Books and feel they have been the perfect fit for us. Thank you, David, Sophie, Ellen, and Georgia, for helping us share our message and for the care and pride you have taken in producing our 'cultural artefact'.

We wish to recognise the dedication and professional work of our graphic designers, Josh and Krysa Allison, co-founders of the independent brand development studio at Staygold. Josh and Krysa have been with us since the beginning. From hearing our initial business ideas, crafting our brand, helping us hone our story and message, to graphically designing countless manifestos for our clients, embracing each of our evolutions, and simply being there for us. They have been an incredibly important and integral part of our journey.

Our heartfelt thanks go out to our **my manifesto** mates, who are a collection of more than one hundred people (family members, friends, and colleagues) who have actively supported us over the past three years. From the early stages of development, we owe special thanks to those who completed our online trials and co-created their personal manifestos with us. They are: Andrew, Chris, Dan, David, Edwina, Gerry, Jen, Joel, Josh, Krysa, Lisa, Lucy, Mary-Anne, Nicole,

Nikki, Rose, Tamara, Tom, and Xavier. Thank you for your belief, your interest, your ideas, and your support. Thank you also to our blog readers, our social media followers, and our event attendees.

We wish also to formally list and thank our book 'road-testers' who read and worked through early copies of our manuscript and provided us with rich feedback and assisted us to fine-tune our process. We thank our road-testers for their support and for generously providing us with the permission to include excerpts of their responses in our book as helpful case studies for fellow readers. Our heartfelt thanks to: Amanda, Charlie, Faith, Jen, Jo, Jon, Kat, Kim, Lennon, Maddy, Nicole, Paula, Pip, Rosa, Syndi, Tony, and Tunya.

In closing, we wish to formally express our appreciation for one another. Our shared and treasured experience of writing this book together has been a beautiful gift for each of us personally. We have both given and received care, comfort, and inspiration from each other and we hope the warmth and respect of our relationship comes through to our readers.

Appendices

Appendix 1: Frequently Asked Questions (FAQs)

1. Do I have to complete every one of the specified exercises?
No.

Of course, we believe there is significant value within each of the twenty-one exercises, as each of them can contribute to you gaining personal insights. If, however, you find a particular exercise unnecessary or unhelpful for you at the present time, please feel free to move on to the next one.

2. What length should my manifesto be?
Great question! Our answer is that this is completely up to you (which we worry you may not think is a helpful answer!).

From our personal work with clients, the 'record' for the shortest manifesto comes in at two words, and the 'record' for the longest manifesto comes in at 547 words! You are most welcome to fit your own manifesto somewhere between these two records, or you are most welcome to set a new record – if you do, please be sure to contact us and let us know.

What do you think the ideal length would be for you? Are you looking to condense your personal insights into one or two memorable sentences that can become something you can memorise and repeat to yourself at specific times? Alternatively, are you looking to put into words a comprehensive expression of what is important to you and the direction you wish to head? With a longer version, you may choose to refer to a particular phrase or paragraph at certain times across your week or month, or you may choose to re-read it when faced with weighty decisions or when considering future directions.

You can be comforted that you will always have your 'raw material' (pages 219–20) and you can select, combine, integrate, or synthesise this material into a current, unique, personal manifesto whenever you choose.

3. Is there an ideal length of time I should take to work through this book?
While there will be personal preferences, we do think there are optimal time frames within which you complete this unique, 7-step process.

Let's start with the quickest time. If you are feeling the vibe and you have the time and headspace, we have known individuals to work through the seven steps over a concentrated day or a dedicated weekend. So, as long as you feel you aren't rushing your responses or reflections, feel free to simply keep going!

As we consider the slowest optimal time, we do know some well-intentioned clients who lost momentum and found that they had breaks that were too long between steps. For some, pacing the process at one step per month is possible and appropriate, but in general we would recommend a pace of one step per week, or per fortnight – this allows time for personal reflection amongst your regular week, whilst still ensuring you are experiencing healthy progress.

One recommendation we have is for you to schedule time each week (or each day, or each fortnight …) where you can prioritise working through this process. It can be as little as fifteen minutes, or as long as a two-hour session. We encourage you to keep moving forward through the book – we trust you will be thrilled, proud, and excited when you arrive at your 'finished' manifesto.

4. How long will my manifesto last?
Maybe a year, possibly a decade, and perhaps a lifetime.

We intentionally and regularly refer to your 'current, unique, personal manifesto' and the reason we stress 'current' – and suggest that you *date* your manifesto – is that you, your life, and our world will continue to evolve and change.

It is our opinion that the wisdom and personal insights you gain from going through the seven steps will be true to who you are at present and will serve you at this age and stage of your life. Quite possibly, some of this wisdom will remain constant throughout your life, and quite possibly with a new chapter in your life, you will choose to complement, modify, or emphasise different insights in your *next* 'current, unique, personal manifesto'.

For an updated edition of your manifesto, you may wish to work completely through the book and each of the exercises again. Alternatively, you may simply turn to your 'raw material' at the end of Part 2 (pages 219–20), and from this canvas construct a new variation that meets you wherever you are at.

5. Should I talk to trusted others about some of my responses and thoughts?
We have designed this process for you to work independently through each of the steps as you sit with your thoughts, your hopes, and your wisdom. Having said this, we welcome and even encourage you to discuss any insights that arise for you with others. At any time, if you feel that sharing and discussing your thoughts and/or responses will increase your connection with others, please go for it. Also, if you think that the perspective and awareness of trusted others will add to your understanding, then we encourage you to bring these people into your journey through this book.

6. What should I do if I am feeling stuck and don't know what to write?
It is quite okay to feel a bit stuck and to simply sit with this feeling for a period of time. We often find that insights will simply arise during the day as you are carrying out routine tasks. Some people have found going for a walk, or a run, or participating in their favourite form of exercise is a helpful way of reflecting, mulling, and possibly unlocking new insights.

The case studies at the end of each chapter are intentionally included for readers to see the breadth and variety of possible responses – these may be helpful to refer to if you are feeling stuck. Another option is to continue moving forward through the exercises and return to your sticking point at a later date.

We have every confidence that you will discover, or reveal, what feels right for you to write.

7. How can I add some accountability to help me 'finish' my manifesto?

We think this is an important consideration for many people. Life is busy and, despite our best intentions, we can start meaningful projects and find they can remain unfinished. While we believe that completing any of the exercises or reading any of the chapters can assist you to gain new wisdom, we are quietly barracking for you to *keep going* and complete the full, current version of your manifesto.

It can be helpful to schedule time each week to spend on your manifesto – book it in like you do for other important appointments or activities.

It can also be helpful to enlist the support of a close friend or family member. Maybe they are working through their copy of the book and you regularly check-in with one another to share personal updates. Possibly, you set times to catch up with one another and agree on what step you will have completed by the time you meet.

Please don't leave your manifesto incomplete because you don't think it is 'perfect.' That's why we included parts of Chapter 1 – you are not seeking perfection. Whatever you write will be right for you at this stage of your life, and there will always be opportunities for you to add or fine-tune your manifesto should you wish to.

You know you would like to *see* your personal manifesto. What would most help you to proudly arrive at this point by a particular date? Go well!

8. Should my manifesto be more about myself or more about others?

Another really interesting question. Your manifesto will help serve *you* to live your authentic life. If what you feel you need most at the moment is to release yourself from particular fears or to harness your positive qualities, or to live in accordance with your values, then you may choose to emphasise words and phrases which gently support and nourish you.

For a different person, or for yourself at a different stage of life, you may choose to focus more on the contribution you can make to your loved ones and your community, along with the connections you wish to strengthen with others.

For many, their personal manifesto is a blend of self and others, but we want you to know that whatever blend or focus feels important for you at this time will be right for you!

9. I want to do 'the work', but I just never feel in the right mood. What can I do?

We get this! But when you don't feel in the mood, sometimes – counter-intuitively – sitting down, opening the book, reading a few pages, and pondering an exercise will get you in the mood. It's worth a try!

Sometimes a particular environment will help you evoke the right mood for you. Maybe it is a quiet reflective place in your home, maybe it is in outside in nature, maybe it is within your favourite café amongst the happy hum of fellow humans, maybe it's your local library. Possibly, you don't need a full environment change – simply getting your cuppa, popping on some music, and picking up your special pen is the set of triggers that readies you for your next productive sitting.

10. Can you (Sue and Justin) coach me to complete my manifesto?
We can! If this is something that appeals to you, please go to our website (mymanifesto.me) for more information.

11. Can I go through the process of completing my manifesto as part of a group of interested people?
You can! If this is something that appeals to you, please go to our website (mymanifesto.me) for more information regarding joining an online cohort or attending one of our retreats.

Appendix 2: The VIA Classification Of Character Strengths

Appreciation of beauty and excellence
Noticing and appreciating beauty, excellence, and/or skilled performance in various domains of life, from nature to art to mathematics to science to everyday experience.

Bravery
Not shrinking from threat, challenge, difficulty, or pain; speaking up for what's right even if there's opposition; acting on convictions even if unpopular; includes physical bravery but is not limited to it.

Creativity
Thinking of novel and productive ways to conceptualise and do things; includes artistic achievement but is not limited to it.

Curiosity
Taking an interest in ongoing experience for its own sake; finding subjects and topics fascinating; exploring and discovering.

Fairness
Treating all people the same according to notions of fairness and justice; not letting feelings bias decisions about others; giving everyone a fair chance.

Forgiveness
Forgiving those who have done wrong; accepting others' shortcomings; giving people a second chance; not being vengeful.

Gratitude
Being aware of and thankful for the good things that happen; taking time to express thanks.

Honesty
Speaking the truth but more broadly presenting oneself in a genuine way and acting in a sincere way; being without pretence; taking responsibility for one's feelings and actions.

Hope
Expecting the best in the future and working to achieve it; believing that a good future is something that can be brought about.

Humility
Letting one's accomplishments speak for themselves; not regarding oneself as more special than one is.

Humour
Liking to laugh and tease; bringing smiles to other people; seeing the light side; making (not necessarily telling) jokes.

Judgement
Thinking things through and examining them from all sides; not jumping to conclusions; being able to change one's mind in light of evidence; weighing all evidence fairly.

Kindness
Doing favours and good deeds for others; helping them; taking care of them.

Leadership
Encouraging a group of which one is a member to get things done and at the same time maintain good relations within the group; organising group activities and seeing that they happen.

Love
Valuing close relations with others, in particular those in which sharing and caring are reciprocated; being close to people.

Love of learning
Mastering new skills, topics, and bodies of knowledge, whether on one's own or formally; related to the strength of curiosity but goes beyond it to describe the tendency to add systematically to what one knows.

Perseverance
Finishing what one starts; persevering in a course of action in spite of obstacles; 'getting it out the door'; taking pleasure in completing tasks.

Perspective
Being able to provide wise counsel to others; having ways of looking at the world that make sense to oneself and others.

Prudence
Being careful about one's choices; not taking undue risks; not saying or doing things that might later be regretted.

Self-regulation
Regulating what one feels and does; being disciplined; controlling one's appetites and emotions.

Social intelligence
Being aware of the motives and feelings of others and oneself; knowing what to do to fit into different social situations; knowing what makes other people tick.

Spirituality
Having coherent beliefs about the higher purpose and meaning of the universe; knowing where one fits within the larger scheme; having beliefs about the meaning of life that shape conduct and provide comfort.

Teamwork
Working well as a member of a group or team; being loyal to the group; doing one's share.

Zest
Approaching life with excitement and energy; not doing things halfway or half-heartedly; living life as an adventure; feeling alive and activated.

Appendix 3: An Overview Of Ten Key Positive Emotions

Joy
Joy derives from the child within us; it is the unfettered rush of good feelings that promises to burst forth at any moment in spontaneous laughter.

Gratitude
Gratitude is warmth of the heart: it arises from an awareness that something good has happened because of a quality we may possess, an action from another, or a tick from the universe.

Contentment
Contentment, or serenity, is a state of being enough, of being happy within oneself and one's circumstances.

Curiosity
Curiosity is the insatiable desire to know, to explore, to question, and is therefore the spark for new learning.

Hope
Hope is the polar opposite of despair; it is the little flame within that refuses to be extinguished.

Pride
Pride is the swelling of the chest that follows achievement: I did that!

Amusement
Amusement is the sense of the absurdity of so much of our behaviour and circumstance; to feel it is to have a degree of unattachment.

Inspiration
Inspiration is the intake of breath when witnessing nobility of sentiment or deed; to glimpse greatness.

Awe
Awe accompanies an awareness of things beyond our imaginings; *this* is possible?

Love
Love is the apotheosis of good feelings; it fills, it generates, it radiates.

Appendix 4: Character Strengths 360 Exercise

Dear _____,

Could I please ask you a favour? It will take you about five minutes to complete. I am currently working through a book that describes a 7-Step guide to creating a personal manifesto. One of the topics covered within this book is raising the awareness of my Character Strengths.

As part of my 'homework', I am encouraged to complete a Character Strengths 360 exercise, where we ask family, friends, and colleagues representing different aspects of my life to provide feedback on the Character Strengths you recognise in me. It feels a bit awkward randomly asking you to give me feedback on my highest Character Strengths, but it is greatly appreciated!

Below are twenty-four Character Strengths, with a brief description of each. Could you please suggest **five** of these Character Strengths which you feel **most strongly** describes me as a person and how I operate in your life? Or, in other words, the five Character Strengths you **most clearly** see in me.

Creativity: Ingenuity; sees and does things in new or unique ways; original and adaptive ideas.

Curiosity: Novelty-seeker; takes an interest; open to different experiences; asks questions.

Judgment: Critical thinker; analytical; logical; thinks things through.

Love of learning: Masters new skills and topics; passionate about knowledge and learning.

Perspective: Wise; provides wise counsel; sees the big picture; integrates others' views.

Bravery: Valorous; does not shrink from fear; speaks up for what's right.

Perseverance: Persistent; industrious; overcomes obstacles; finishes what is started.

Honesty: Integrity; truthful; authentic.

Zest: Enthusiastic; energetic; vital; feels alive and activated.

Love: Gives and accepts love; genuine; values close relations with others.

Kindness: Generous; nurturing; caring; compassionate; altruistic; nice.

Teamwork: A team player; community-focused; socially responsible; loyal.

Fairness: Just; does not allow feelings to bias decisions about others.

Leadership: Organises group activities; encourages and leads groups to get things done.

Forgiveness: Merciful; accepts others' shortcomings; gives people a second chance.

Humility: Modest; lets accomplishments speak for themselves; focuses on others.

Prudence: Careful; wisely cautious; thinks before speaking; does not take undue risks.

Self-regulation: Self-controlled; disciplined; manages impulses and emotions.

Appreciation of beauty and excellence: Awe; wonder; marvels at beauty and greatness.

Spirituality: Religious and/or spiritual; practices a faith; purpose- and meaning-driven.

Gratitude: Thankful for the good; expresses thanks; feels blessed.

Hope: Optimistic; future-minded; has a positive outlook.

Humour: Playful; enjoys joking and bringing smiles to others; light-hearted.

Social intelligence: Aware of the motives and feelings of oneself and others; knows what makes other people tick.

If possible, simply write down the names of the five Character Strengths and provide a brief rationale or example of how you have seen me display this strength.

Many thanks,

_____

P.S. Please let me know if you would like me to return the favour and share with you the Character Strengths that I see in you!

Appendix 5: 50+ Authentic Living Books That We Love

Mike Bayer, **Best Self**

Tal Ben-Shahar, **Being Happy, Happiness Studies**

Warren Berger, **A More Beautiful Question**

Susan Biggar, **The Upside of Down**

Richard Boyatzis, Melvin Smith, Ellen Van Oosten, **Helping People Change**

Brene Brown, **Rising Strong, Daring to Lead, Atlas of the Heart**

Michael Bungay Stanier, **The Coaching Habit**

Oliver Burkeman, **The Antidote**

James Clear, **Atomic Habits**

Ayelet Fishbach, **Get It Done**

Viktor Frankl, **Man's Search for Meaning, Yes to Life**

Robert Fulghum, **All I Really Need to Know I Learned in Kindergarten**

Maureen Gaffney, **Flourishing**

Elizabeth Gilbert, **Big Magic**

Seth Godin, **The Dip**

Russ Harris, **The Happiness Trap**

Donna Hicks, **Dignity**

Ryan Holiday, **The Daily Stoic, The Obstacle is the Way, Courage is Calling**

Kerry Howells, **Untangling You**

Gerald Jampolsky, **Love is Letting go of Fear**

Matthew Johnstone, **The Big Little Book of Resilience**

Stephen Joseph, **What Doesn't Kill Us**

Austin Kleon, **Steal Like an Artist**

Roman Krznaric, **The Good Ancestor**

William Macaskill, **Doing Good Better**

Hugh Mackay, **The Inner Self, Australia Reimagined**

Chris Mackey, **The Positive Psychology of Synchronicity**

Robert Maurer, **One Small Step Can Change Your Life**

Wayne McCashen, **The Strengths Approach**

Kellie McGonigal, **The Upside of Stress, The Joy of Exercise**

Mark McKergow, **The Next Generation of Solution Focused Practice**

Adam Morgan & Mark Barden, **A beautiful constraint**

Kristin Neff, **Self-compassion, Fierce Self-compassion**

Kristi Nelson, **Wake Up Grateful**

Ryan Niemiec, **Mindfulness and Character Strengths**

Chris Peterson, **Pursuing the Good Life**

Dan Pink, **Drive, The Power of Regret**

Ken Robinson, **Finding Your Element**

Martin Seligman, **Flourish**

Maria Sirois, **A Short Course in Happiness After Loss**

Bronnie Ware, **The Top Five Regrets of the Dying**

John Whitmore, **Coaching for Performance**

Brianna Wiest, **The Mountain is You**

Rosamund and Benjamin Zander, **The Art of Possibility**

Appendix 6: Some Inspirational Words

As you are refining your words and making your manifesto sing, consider whether any of these listed words would inspire and lift you. Sometimes you may know what you want to say but haven't quite found the best word to say it. Could it be one of these words?

Abundance
Adventure/adventurous
Aesthetic
Agency
Aligning
Anchored
Appreciative/appreciate
Aspire/aspiration
Authenticity/authentic
Awakens/awake
Awe
Beauty
Belonging
Benefit
Blessing
Bounty/bounteous
Capabilities
Captivates
Catalyst
Chaos
Character
Cherish
Cherished
Collaborator
Colourful
Compassion/self-compassion
Competency
Complement
Complexity
Connectedness
Connection/connectedness
Consideration
Continuous
Continuum
Contributing/contribution
Convergence/converging
Courage/courageously
Creative
Crucible
Cultivate
Curious
Distinctive
Duality
Earthing
Emanate
Embodies
Embrace
Empathic/empathy
Enables
Encounter
Endeavour
Endless
Energising
Enlivened
Enrichment
Ethical
Ever-present
Exceptional
Extension
Facilitate
Facilitating/facilitation
Flourish
Foster
Foundation
Fragile
Fulfilled/fulfilment
Fun-loving
Generous/generosity
Gifter/gifting
Goodness
Govern
Grace
Grant
Growth
Harmony
Healing
Heart-centre
Honourable
Humanity
Humility
Immerse
Imperatives
Incandescent
Ineffable/ineffability
Innate
Innovation/innovative
Inquisitive
Insatiable
Integral

Integrate/integration
Integrity
Intent/intention
Intentional/intentionally/intentionality
Interact/interaction
Interaction/actions
Intuition/intuitively
Judicious
Levity
Liberation/liberated
Life-long
Lightly
Limitless/unlimited
Lodestar
Mantle
Measure/measured
Metaphor
Microcosm/macrocosm
Mystery
Nurtures/nurturing
Oneness
Open-hearted/wholehearted
Opportunities
Paradox
Paramount
Passionate
Perforce
Perspectives
Philosophy
Planetary/planet
Platform
Playfully
Possibilities
Precious
Prevails
Pristine
Protection/protectiveness
Purpose/purposeful
Quell
Radiant
Realignment
Refined/refine
Reflect/reflection
Rekindle
Reliant
Resolve
Responsible
Revelations
Ripple
Safeguard
Savour
Sensorial/senses
Sentient
Service
Shelter
Solace
Spiritual
Steadfast
Stretch
Surety
Talents
Tangible
Temper/temperance
Traits
Transcendence/transcends
Transform/transformative/transformational
Unafraid
Unconditional
Understanding
Unfold/unfolding
Unique/uniqueness
Values-driven
Vision
Vital
Voracious/voraciously
Vulnerability/vulnerable
Well-adjusted
Wellspring
Wondrous/wonder/wonderful/wonderment
Wordsmith
Zest-filled

Sue's Current Manifesto

I replenish myself and navigate all that life presents with love, including self-love.

I deeply value authenticity in all my interactions and seek the bravery I need to live in integrity.

I allow myself the right to construct the meanings by which I live.

I aim to continue to grow spiritually and to contribute my ideas to the world.

I am a human being with all the complexity and flaws of every other human being; I release myself from trying to be more.

My hoped-for role is of a leader, who has lived a full life and is prepared to share the benefits of what I have learned.

I wish to create a community of care throughout my immediate family, my community, and the society of which I am one.

Justin's Current Manifesto

I actively seek to live a balanced life – where I am present, hands-on, supportive, and loving towards my wife, my children, my family, and my close friends.

And, where I am highly engaged in creating experiences for many others that enable them to be well and to live into their authentic lives.

My Signature Strengths of perseverance and kindness, energise me to show up with compassion and care for people and for projects.

I strive to cultivate courage, expressing myself clearly and bravely standing up for others.

I wish to show respect, humility, generosity, and grace to all. I love to grow, and I welcome adventure into my life.